and eventually disposed of can result in the increased usage of finite resources/environmental damage linked to the collection of resources *[2 marks]*.

b) E.g. newer power tools are likely to have more efficient components than older power tools *[1 mark]*. This means they may have lower carbon footprints *[1 mark]*.

4 a) Re-use:
Disposable plastic razor: e.g. the design could be changed so the main body is reused and just the head with the blades is thrown away *[1 mark]*. This would reduce the amount of energy and plastic being used *[1 mark]*.
Stuffed toy: e.g. the stuffing could be made of material left-over from making other products *[1 mark]*. Less new material would be used making it *[1 mark]*.

b) Refuse:
Disposable plastic razor: e.g. the customer could refuse to buy a disposable product and buy a razor where just the blades change *[1 mark]*. Fewer razors would be thrown away so it would reduce the amount of waste *[1 mark]*.
Stuffed toy: e.g. the customer could refuse to buy a toy not made from non-finite resources, e.g. cotton *[1 mark]*. Fewer finite resources would be used making the toy *[1 mark]*.

c) Reduce:
Disposable plastic razor: e.g. the razor should be redesigned to use less material *[1 mark]*. This would save resources and energy *[1 mark]*.
Stuffed toy: e.g. less stuffing could be used in each toy *[1 mark]*. Less material would be used, saving resources and energy *[1 mark]*.

5 E.g. when plant materials are used to make the bioplastic more can be planted to replace them/plant material is a non-finite resource *[1 mark]* whereas, oil-based plastic is made from a finite resource *[1 mark]*. / When the bioplastic toothbrush is disposed of at the end of its life it can breakdown fully *[1 mark]* rather than taking up space in landfill like an oil-based plastic toothbrush *[1 mark]*.

Remember that finite resources can also be called non-renewable resources and non-finite resources can be called renewable resources. It's easy to confuse them, so double check you've written the one you meant to if you mention them in an answer to an exam question.

Pages 11-12 — Products in Society

1 A *[1 mark]*
2 B *[1 mark]*
3 D *[1 mark]*
4 C *[1 mark]*
5 Any two from: e.g. they could promote the range on social media. / They could promote the range via email. / They could get the range moved nearer the top of the page in search engine results *[2 marks]*.

6 a) E.g. when new products are designed, or existing ones are improved, as a result of new technology or manufacturing techniques *[1 mark]*.

b) i) E.g. the new model has a larger screen *[1 mark]* because technology has improved so larger screens can be used *[1 mark]*. / The new model is thinner *[1 mark]* because screen and other computer technology has decreased in size to allow this thinness *[1 mark]*. / The new model has a touchscreen instead of a keyboard *[1 mark]* because of advances in screen technology *[1 mark]*.

ii) E.g. the new model has a larger screen *[1 mark]* because people want to be able to comfortably watch videos etc. on their smartphone *[1 mark]*. / The new model is thinner *[1 mark]* because people want phones that are less bulky to carry around *[1 mark]*.

Some of the differences between the phones could have been caused by technology push or market pull, as manufacturers continually redesign products in response to both of these things. So as long as you explain your reasoning, these differences can be valid answer for either part i) or ii).

7 a) E.g. elderly people / people with a disability *[1 mark]*.

b) Large buttons: e.g. large buttons are easier to use for elderly people with less ⬚ *[1 mark]*.
High ringing volu⬚ ...⬚⬚⬚ ...⬚⬚⬚ volume is suited to elderly people / people with a hearing impairment that need the phone to ring loudly so they can hear it *[1 mark]*.
Ability to make the on-screen text larger: e.g. being able to increase the size of text is suited to elderly people / people with a vision impairment who will find it easier to read larger text *[1 mark]*.

Pages 13-14 — Powering Systems

Warm-up
Renewable: solar, tidal, wind, biomass, hydroelectricity
Non-renewable: coal, oil, gas, nuclear fuel

1 E.g. a non-renewable energy resource will one day run out *[1 mark]* but a renewable energy resource can be renewed as it is used *[1 mark]*.
2 D *[1 mark]*
3 C *[1 mark]*
4 a) E.g. wind turbines can be noisy *[1 mark]* / wind turbines can spoil the landscape/look ugly *[1 mark]*.

b) E.g. solar panels only produce electricity in the daytime whereas wind turbines can produce electricity through the night *[1 mark]*.

5 Any two from: e.g. they're finite so will eventually run out. / Their extraction has negative social and environmental impacts. / They release greenhouse gases when they are burned, which causes lots of environmental problems *[2 marks]*.

6 a) i) E.g. from 1995 to 2015, the production of electricity from renewable resources increased, from 0.2 to 1.6 TWh *[1 mark]*.

ii) E.g. extracting and burning fossil fuels damages the environment. / Many people think it's better to learn to get by without non-renewables before they run out. / Improved efficiency in renewable power production mean renewables are becoming a more attractive option. / Governments have begun to introduce targets for using more renewable resources, and for cutting down on carbon dioxide emissions *[1 mark]*.

b) i) 2015: 3.0 + 1.6 = 4.6 TWh
1995: 3.8 + 0.2 = 4.0 TWh
4.6 − 4.0 = 0.6 TWh
[2 marks for a correct answer, otherwise 1 mark for correctly calculating the electricity produced each year.]

To get the right data from the graph to use in these calculations, you need to make sure you've worked out the scale of the y-axis (the vertical axis). In this question each square on the y-axis is equal to 0.1 TWh because there are 10 squares for every 1.0 TWh (1.0 ÷ 10 = 0.1). For example, this means that six squares up from 1.0 is equal to 1.6 TWh.

ii) E.g. the population may have increased / the number of electronic devices that people own/use may have increased *[1 mark]*.

Section Two — An Introduction to Materials and Systems

Page 15 — Properties of Materials

Warm-up
Toughness — The ability of a material to change shape instead of breaking or snapping.
Hardness — The ability to withstand scratching, abrasion or denting.
Density — A measure of the mass per unit volume of a material.

1 C *[1 mark]*
2 B *[1 mark]*

Electrical wires need to be good electrical conductors, so electricity can flow through them easily.

3 a) E.g. it's the ability of a material to let heat travel through it *[1 mark]*.

b) Any two from: e.g. they have high melting points/low fusibility / they are malleable *[2 marks]*

Pages 16-17 — Paper, Board and Timber

Warm-up
Softwood — pine, larch, spruce
Hardwood — oak, mahogany, beech, balsa, ash

Section Two

1   D *[1 mark]*
2   D *[1 mark]*
3   Property: e.g. high strength-to-weight ratio / low density / soft
     [1 mark]
     Use: e.g. modelling *[1 mark]*
4   Any two from: e.g. it has attractive grain markings / it finishes
     well / it is durable / it is tough / it is very strong *[2 marks]*.
5   E.g. hardwood tends to be denser than softwood *[1 mark]* and
     hardwood tends to be harder than softwood *[1 mark]*.
6   Use: e.g. decking / fence posts *[1 mark]*
     Property: e.g. hard / tough / durable / resistant to rot *[1 mark]*
*Resistance to rot is a useful property for wood that is used outside because it
will be exposed to moisture.*
7   B *[1 mark]*
8 a) e.g. duplex board *[1 mark]*
  b) E.g. duplex board can have a different colour on each side (as
     shown in Figure 1) / has a smooth surface on one side, which
     allows the packaging to be printed on (as shown in Figure 1)
     [1 mark].

Pages 18-19 — Metals, Alloys and Polymers

1   B *[1 mark]*
2   A *[1 mark]*
3   E.g. it's ductile *[1 mark]* and a good electrical conductor
     [1 mark].
4   Any two from: e.g. strong / corrosion-resistant / malleable /
     looks good (has a nice colour) *[2 marks]*
5   E.g. drilling materials at high speed generates heat *[1 mark]*.
     High speed steel keeps its hardness when heated to high
     temperatures *[1 mark]*.
*If cutting implements such as drill bits are not as hard as the material that is
being cut, the bit will be cut away instead.*
6   B *[1 mark]*
7   C *[1 mark]*
*Phenol-formaldehyde is very easily moulded into bottle caps,
snooker balls, etc.*
8 a) Plastic — e.g. high-density polyethylene / HDPE *[1 mark]*.
     Reason — e.g. it's stiff so will keep its shape / it's strong so it
     can carry things without breaking / it's lightweight so it is easy to
     carry things *[1 mark]*.
  b) Plastic — e.g. polyvinyl chloride / PVC *[1 mark]*.
     Reason — e.g. it's cheap so it can be used in mass production /
     it's durable so offers long-lasting protective packaging *[1 mark]*.
  c) Plastic — e.g. polyethylene terephthalate / PET *[1 mark]*
     Reason — e.g. it's light so is good for being carried around /
     it's strong so will withstand being knocked or squashed without
     breaking / it's tough so will bend a little rather than breaking
     [1 mark].

Pages 20-21 — Textiles

1   B *[1 mark]*
2   A *[1 mark]*
*Sportswear is commonly made from synthetic fibres such as elastane, polyester
and polyamide.*
3   A *[1 mark]*
4   E.g. natural fibres are easier to dye/more absorbent than
     synthetic fibres *[1 mark]*. Natural fibres have less resistance to
     biological damage than synthetic fibres *[1 mark]*.
5   D *[1 mark]*
A 2-ply yarn is made up of two yarns twisted together.
6   Fibre: polyamide *[1 mark]*
     Property: e.g. strong / hard-wearing / warm / good elasticity
     / crease-resistant / resists biological damage / fairly cheap
     [1 mark]
7 a) elastane *[1 mark]*
  b) Any three from: e.g. it's soft / extremely elastic / strong / hard-
     wearing / lightweight / keeps its shape well / resists sun / resists
     biological damage / non-absorbent / highly flammable / not
     biodegradable *[3 marks]*.
  c) E.g. sportswear / underwear *[1 mark]*.
8 a) Any two from: e.g. warm / crease-resistant / can be lightweight /
     good elasticity *[2 marks]*.

  b) Any two from: e.g. it can shrink when washed / it can feel itchy /
     it can be fairly expensive / it dries slowly *[2 marks]*.

Pages 22-23 — Textiles and Manufactured Boards

Warm-up
A: woven, B: non-woven, C: knitted
1   B *[1 mark]*
2   E.g. webs of synthetic fibres *[1 mark]* that are either glued,
     needle-punched, stitched or melted together *[1 mark]*.
3   Any two from: e.g. strong / hard-wearing / not very
     absorbent / soft / resistant to creasing / doesn't shrink
     easily / highly flammable *[2 marks]*.
4   C *[1 mark]*
*The weft yarn travels from right to left across the weave, and the warp yarn
travels up and down the weave.*
5   B *[1 mark]*
*The layers of wood are arranged so that the grain directions are at 90° to the
layers above and below.*
6   A blended fabric is made from a yarn that is a combination of
     two or more different types of fibre *[1 mark]*. A mixed fabric is
     made from two or more different types of yarn *[1 mark]*.
7 a) chipboard *[1 mark]*
  b) e.g. self-assembly furniture *[1 mark]*
8   E.g. it's cheap *[1 mark]*, so it will save money for the charity
     [1 mark]. / It has a smooth finish *[1 mark]*, which is good for
     printing the logo on *[1 mark]*.
9   Name: e.g. MDF *[1 mark]*
     Reasoning: E.g. it's a cheap material, so it's suitable for flat-pack
     furniture, which is generally sold cheaply *[1 mark]*. It has a
     smooth uniform surface, so it can take paint well *[1 mark]*.

Pages 24-26 — Electronic Systems

Warm-up

Component	Circuit symbol
Battery	—┤ ╎ ├—
Switch	—o ⌿o—
Resistor	—⊏▭⊐—
Thermistor	—⊏▱⊐—
Light-dependent resistor (LDR)	⊖
Buzzer	⟕
Bulb	—⊗—

1   A *[1 mark]*
2 a) a buzzer *[1 mark]*
  b) e.g. a light-emitting diode / LED *[1 mark]*
3   25 °C *[1 mark]*
*Reading off the graph, this is the temperature at which the resistance of the
thermistor is 10 000 ohms.*
4   B *[1 mark]*
A voltage pushes an electrical current around a circuit.
5   C *[1 mark]*
6 a) E.g. a microcontroller programmed as a timer could be used
     [1 mark]. This device could be used to add a set time delay to
     the system, for example, from when the light is turned on until it
     is due to be turned off *[1 mark]*.
  b) Input device: e.g. light-dependent resistor (LDR) *[1 mark]*
     Reason: e.g. it senses changes in light levels, so could switch the
     circuit on when it gets dark enough *[1 mark]*.
7   Any two from: e.g. using ICs simplifies the electronic system
     / systems with ICs are cheaper to make / systems with ICs are
     smaller / systems with ICs use much less power *[2 marks]*.
8   C *[1 mark]*
*In NOT logic gates, if the input is on, the output will be off and if the input is
off, the output is on.*
9 a) an OR logic gate *[1 mark]*
  b) E.g. if one input or the other (or both) is on then the output is
     also on *[1 mark]*.
10   B *[1 mark]*
11 a) i) sensor *[1 mark]*
     ii) LCD display *[1 mark]*
   b) It counts pulses of voltage produced by an input device *[1 mark]*.

Section Three

Pages 27-29 — Mechanical Systems
Warm-up

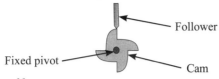

1   C *[1 mark]*
The gear ratio can be written as
"no. of teeth on driven gear : no. of teeth on driver gear" — 45 : 15 here.
The ratio can be simplified to 3 : 1 by dividing both sides by 15.
2 a) bell crank *[1 mark]*
   b) It changes the direction of a force through 90° *[1 mark]*
3 a) first order lever *[1 mark]*
   b) E.g. it gives a mechanical advantage meaning the nail can be removed with a small effort *[1 mark]*.
4   D *[1 mark]*
5   D *[1 mark]*
6   E.g. changing the size of the cam *[1 mark]*. Changing the shape of the cam *[1 mark]*.
7 a) idler gear *[1 mark]*
   b) Clockwise *[1 mark]* because the idler gear/gear A is turned anticlockwise *[1 mark]*.
   c) Slower *[1 mark]* because gear B is larger with more teeth than the driver gear *[1 mark]*.
8   B *[1 mark]*
9   C *[1 mark]*
10   velocity ratio = 105 ÷ 35 = 3/1 / 3:1 / 3 *[1 mark]*

Pages 30-31 — Development in New Materials
1   C *[1 mark]*
2   A *[1 mark]*
3   D *[1 mark]*
4 a) Materials made of tiny particles/nanoparticles *[1 mark]*.
   b) E.g.
       Carbon nanotubes *[1 mark]* are used in tennis racquets / electronics *[1 mark]*.
       Antibacterial fabrics *[1 mark]* are used in face masks / dressings / toys / odour-free socks *[1 mark]*.
5 a) E.g. shape memory alloy/nitinol / photochromic pigments *[1 mark]*.
   b) E.g.
       Shape memory alloy/nitinol:
       If you deform products made from this, they can be returned to their original shape by heating *[1 mark]*, so frames made from this can be easily fixed if they get accidentally bent out of shape *[1 mark]*.
       Photochromic pigment:
       It can change colour when exposed to different levels of light *[1 mark]*, so sunglasses with photochromic lenses can be designed to get darker in bright light, and clearer in low light *[1 mark]*.
6   D *[1 mark]*
7 a) A material formed by bonding two or more different materials together *[1 mark]*.
   b) Any two from: e.g. it is light / it is tough / it is strong *[2 marks]*.
8   E.g. thermochromic pigments *[1 mark]* as these change colour in response to heat *[1 mark]*.

Section Three — More about Materials

Pages 32-33 — Selecting Materials
Warm-up
False, True, False
1 a) A duty to act in a way that benefits society and the environment *[1 mark]*.
   b) E.g. they are often cheaper than socially responsible design choices *[1 mark]*.
2 a) Any two from: e.g. the material needs to be strong enough to support the weight of items that will be put on it / it needs to be lightweight so the table is portable / it must be able to withstand outdoor conditions *[2 marks]*.
   b) Any two from: e.g. colour / surface finishes / texture *[2 marks]*.
   c) E.g. materials that are widely available are usually less expensive / quicker and easier to source *[1 mark]*.
   d) E.g. buying the materials in bulk allows the company to negotiate a discount with the supplier *[1 mark]*. This means the table can be made for less money, so can be sold for a cheaper price *[1 mark]*.
3 a) A material that is produced in an environmentally sustainable way *[1 mark]* that is also fair to workers *[1 mark]*.
   b) E.g. it has come from responsibly managed forests and/or verified recycled sources *[1 mark]*.
   c) i) Re-used metals are used again for the same purpose as they were originally made for *[1 mark]*. Recycled metals are used again for a different purpose *[1 mark]*.
      ii) E.g. they would help to limit the amount of metal on rubbish tips *[1 mark]* and the amount of metal ore that would need to be mined to make the bed frames *[1 mark]*.

Pages 34-35 — Forces and Stresses
1 a) torsion *[1 mark]*
   b) shear *[1 mark]*
2 a) Extra layers of fabric that are stuck/sewn onto the inside of textiles products *[1 mark]*.
   b) Any two from: e.g. they add strength to the collar / they add rigidity to the collar / they improve the functionality of the collar / they improve the aesthetics of the collar *[2 marks]*.
   c) e.g. cuffs / pockets / button holes *[1 mark]*
3 a) Force A: tension *[1 mark]*
       Force B: bending *[1 mark]*
   b) i) E.g. a woven fabric *[1 mark]* with a high tensile strength *[1 mark]*.
      ii) E.g. webbing has a high tensile strength, so it won't break easily when the straps are under tension/when the hammock is in use *[1 mark]*.
4 a) It is laminated/layered *[1 mark]*. The middle layer is made up of a series of bends *[1 mark]*.
   b) E.g. strength is important as it means the packaging is less likely to break under the weight *[1 mark]*. Rigidity is important, because it allows the packaging to hold its shape better *[1 mark]*.
   c) It is less rigid *[1 mark]*.

Pages 36-37 — Scales of Production
1 a) E.g. products are made to exactly meet their requirements *[1 mark]*.
   b) E.g. they are labour-intensive/can take a long time to make *[1 mark]* and often require highly skilled labour *[1 mark]*.
2 a) Production that goes for 24 hours a day without stopping at any point *[1 mark]*.
   b) E.g. the process can be made very efficient / the cost per item is low *[1 mark]*.
   c) e.g. aluminium foil / chemicals *[1 mark]*
3 a) Products that are identical to each other *[1 mark]* and that are for the mass-market/bought by lots of people *[1 mark]*.
   b) Any two from: e.g. by replacing the silk with a cheaper fabric / by using artificial pearls / by stitching the pearls on using a machine / by simplifying the pearl design *[2 marks]*.
   c) E.g. it may use expensive specialised equipment *[1 mark]*.
4 a) Type of production: one-off production
       Desk — any two from: e.g. the desk might be made from expensive materials (e.g. solid wood, oak, mahogany or steel) / be hand-made by a skilful worker / have intricate decoration / be custom-made to fit a room/user.
       Formal shoes — any two from: e.g. the shoes might be designed to be made of expensive materials (e.g. leather uppers and soles) / be hand-made by a skilful worker / be hand-stitched / be designed to fit a customer perfectly.
       Earrings — any two from: e.g. the design might use expensive materials (e.g. gold, silver, diamond) / be quite intricate / be hand-made by a skilled worker.
       [2 marks]

Section Three

b) Type of production: batch production *[1 mark]*
Desk — any two from: e.g. they might be designed to be made from slightly cheaper materials (e.g. a hardwood veneer glued to manufactured boards) / have a simpler, standard design / designed to be made using jigs/templates/moulds / be made in a range of standard sizes/veneers/colours / use standard components / use simple decoration.
Formal shoes — any two from: e.g. they might be designed to be made from slightly cheaper materials (lower quality leather or plastic) / have a simpler, standard design / designed to be made using jigs/templates/moulds / be made in a range of standard sizes / use standard components.
Earrings — any two from: e.g. the earrings might have a simpler/less intricate design / designed to be made using jigs/templates/moulds / be made using cheaper materials (e.g. steel, glass, or plastic) / use standard components.
[2 marks]

c) Type of production: mass production *[1 mark]*
Desk — any two from: e.g. they might be made from cheap materials (e.g. plastic laminate glued to manufactured board) / have designs with little or no detail / only be made in one standard size / be flat-packed/self-assembled / use CAD/CAM.
Formal shoes — any two from: e.g. they might be made from cheaper materials (plastic) / have designs with little or no detail/decoration / they will be made in standard sizes / use CAD/CAM.
Earrings — any two from: e.g. they might have a very simple design / be made using only cheaper materials (e.g. steel, plastic) / use CAD/CAM.
[2 marks]

5 a) Batch production *[1 mark]* — e.g. because the machines can be easily altered to produce the different types of bed frame *[1 mark]*.

b) Mass production *[1 mark]* — e.g. because thousands of identical cars will be made / the cars can be made on a production line *[1 mark]*.

Pages 38-39 — Quality Control

1 a) To check products have been made to a high enough standard *[1 mark]* and to make sure they meet the manufacturing specification *[1 mark]*.

b) E.g. it would take too long to test every product/component that was manufactured *[1 mark]*.

2 a) registration mark *[1 mark]*

b) It's used to make sure the printing plates are aligned *[1 mark]*.

3 a) Upper limit — 51 mm *[1 mark]*
Lower limit — 49 mm *[1 mark]*

b) go/no go fixture / limit gauge *[1 mark]*

c) E.g. it is faster than having to measure the actual dimensions of a component *[1 mark]*.

4 a) E.g. check the label has printed clearly / check that it has been cut to the right size / check that the colours have printed correctly *[1 mark]*.

b) i) 27 mm *[1 mark]*
25 mm plus the 2 mm of tolerance.

ii) E.g. that it is stuck on straight / that it is stuck on securely / that it is stuck on the right way up *[1 mark]*.

c) The label is not within the required tolerance *[1 mark]*, because the height should be between 47.5 mm and 52.5 mm (50 ± 2.5 mm) which it is not *[1 mark]*.

5 a) E.g. a depth stop is a long rod that is clamped close to the drill bit *[1 mark]*. Once the chosen depth has been reached, the depth stop comes into contact with the material and prevents the drill from going any deeper *[1 mark]*.

b) E.g. the power settings *[1 mark]* and the feed rate *[1 mark]*.

c) E.g. keeping the PCB exposure times to UV light/the developer solution/the etching solution constant *[1 mark]*.

Pages 40-41 — Production Aids

1 a) A jig helps guide tools when working on a component / a jig makes sure that the workpiece is positioned in the right place *[1 mark]*.

b) Any two from: e.g. it can reduce errors / it makes the pre-drilled holes consistent/identical for each different shelving unit / it saves time/effort *[2 marks]*.

2 a) Sketch of a balloon or a candle shaped template *[1 mark]*.

b) E.g. wood / plastic / metal *[1 mark]* because it is a strong and hard-wearing material *[1 mark]*.
Paper or card would not be used to make the template because they would become worn or damaged if used repeatedly.

c) A template is drawn round with a pencil/cut round on a protective mat with a knife *[1 mark]*.

3 a) The pattern is a template that is pinned to the fabric *[1 mark]* and cut round *[1 mark]*. The cut pieces of fabric are then sewn together to make a textiles product *[1 mark]*.

b) i) e.g. resin / wood / metal *[1 mark]*

ii) E.g. casting patterns can be used many times *[1 mark]* and they make products that are a consistent shape *[1 mark]*.

4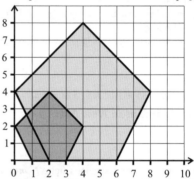
Multiply the initial coordinates by a scale factor of 2: (2,0), (6,0), (8,4), (4,8), (0,4).
[2 marks for correct drawing, otherwise 1 mark for correctly multiplying by a scale factor of 2]
You can check your answer using a ruler — each new coordinate should be twice as far from the datum as the corresponding old coordinate.

Pages 42-43 — Production of Materials

1 a) fractional distillation *[1 mark]*

b) Some fractions need to be broken down into smaller molecules (cracked) before they can be polymerised *[1 mark]*.

2 E.g. seasoned wood would be stronger than unseasoned wood *[1 mark]*. Seasoned wood would be less likely to rot than unseasoned wood *[1 mark]*.

3 a) A rock with enough metal locked up in it *[1 mark]* to make it profitable for the metal to be extracted from the rest of the ore *[1 mark]*.

b) Process: heating the ore in a furnace *[1 mark]*
Metal: e.g. iron / zinc / copper / tin *[1 mark]*
Process: electrolysis *[1 mark]*
Metal: e.g. aluminium / zinc *[1 mark]*

c) To remove any remaining impurities *[1 mark]*.

4 a) E.g. the wood chips are ground down *[1 mark]* to separate out the fibres *[1 mark]* / the wood chips are heated with chemicals *[1 mark]*, which dissolves non-fibrous parts of the wood, leaving only the cellulose fibres behind *[1 mark]*.

b) The pulp is washed and bleached to make it white *[1 mark]*. Then it is pressed flat between rollers, dried and cut to size *[1 mark]*.

c) other plants, e.g. grasses *[1 mark]*

5 Name: plywood *[1 mark]*
How to grade your answer:
[No marks] There is no relevant information.
[1 mark] There is a brief description of the process, but key stages are left out and the answer contains a number of errors. AND/OR there is a diagram but it lacks detail and clarity.
[2 marks] There is a description of the process, but some points are missing or there are some errors. AND/OR there is

Section Four

a diagram with some annotations, but it lacks detail or contains errors.

[3 marks] There is a detailed description of the process, with most stages in the correct order but the description may contain small errors or lack some clarity. AND/OR there is an annotated diagram, which is mainly correct but some points are missing.

[4 marks] There is a clear, accurate and detailed description of the process, including the key stages in the correct order. AND/OR there is an accurate and appropriately annotated diagram clearly showing the process.

Here are some points your answer may include:
The wood is softened through soaking it in hot water or steaming it.
A thin sheet is peeled from the softened wood.
The sheet is cut into a suitable size and dried.
The cut wood is arranged into stacks of three or more, with each layer having a grain direction 90° to the layers above and below.
Glue is added between each layer.
The sheets are heated and pressed.
(Relevant, labelled sketches with annotations showing these points should also be credited.)

Pages 44-45 — More on the Production of Materials

Warm-up
Wool — Sheep's fleece, Silk — The cocoon of a worm,
Nylon — Crude oil

1   Natural fibres — e.g. wool / cotton / silk *[1 mark]*
    Regenerated fibres — e.g. viscose fibres *[1 mark]*
    Synthetic fibres — e.g. polyester / LYCRA® / nylon *[1 mark]*

2 a) i)   Cutting down large areas of forest without planting new trees to replace the old ones *[1 mark]*.
     ii)   E.g. deforestation destroys forest habitats *[1 mark]*, which has a negative impact on the plants and animals that live there *[1 mark]*.
   b)   E.g. mining uses a lot of energy from fossil fuels, which can cause air pollution/contribute to global warming / large areas of land are cleared for mining, which leads to the destruction of habitats / chemicals and waste rock can pollute nearby water, and harm wildlife *[1 mark]*.

3 a)   Cotton — cotton plant *[1 mark]*
    Polyester — crude oil *[1 mark]*
   b) i)   E.g. farming for cotton fibres often uses artificial fertilisers/pesticides, which can pollute rivers and harm wildlife *[1 mark]*. Land may need to be cleared for farming, which could involve deforestation/clearing of habitats *[1 mark]*.
     ii)   Any two from: e.g. drilling for crude oil can result in toxic chemicals being released into the atmosphere / can result in waste material/oil leaks, which pollute the surrounding habitats / may require land to be cleared to make room for the drill site, which can destroy habitats *[2 marks]*.
   c)   How to grade your answer:
    [No marks] There is no relevant information.
    [1 mark] There is a brief description of the process, but key stages are left out and the answer contains a number of errors. AND/OR there is a diagram but it lacks detail and clarity.
    [2 marks] There is a description of the process, but some points are missing or there are some errors. AND/OR there is a diagram with some annotations, but it lacks detail or contains errors.
    [3 marks] There is a detailed description of the process, with most stages in the correct order but the description may contain small errors or lack some clarity. AND/OR there is an annotated diagram, which is mainly correct but some points are missing.
    [4 marks] There is a clear, accurate and detailed description of the process, including the key stages in the correct order. AND/OR there is an accurate and appropriately annotated diagram clearly showing the process.
    Here are some points your answer may include:
    Cotton:
    The plants are treated with chemicals to make the leaves fall off.
    The cotton fibres are then harvested.

The cotton fibres are cleaned to remove dirt.
The seeds are removed from the pods.
The fibres are then combed using wire rollers (carding).
The fibres are then spun into yarn.
Polyester:
Crude oil is fractionally distilled.
Certain fractions are polymerised to make a polymer (polyester).
The polymer is then melted and forced through tiny holes to form long filaments.
The filaments are left to cool, before being spun into yarn.
(Relevant, labelled sketches with annotations showing these points should also be credited.)

Section Four — Paper and Board

Pages 46-47 — Properties of Paper and Board

Warm-up
false, false, true

1 a)   Flyers and leaflets don't need to last for a long time *[1 mark]*.
   b)   e.g. low-weight / biodegradable / unbleached *[1 mark]*
2 a) i)   A6 paper *[1 mark]*
     ii)   A2 paper *[1 mark]*
   b)   area = 1 ÷ 8 = 0.125 m² *[1 mark]*

A3 paper is 8 times smaller than A0 so that's why you divide the area of an A0 sheet by 8.

3 a)   Type of paper/board: e.g. board laminated with aluminium *[1 mark]*
    Reasons: e.g. it's airtight, so it keeps flavour in and air out. Advertising and nutritional information can be printed onto the paper. *[Maximum 2 marks, 1 for each correct reason]*.
   b)   Type of paper/board: e.g. corrugated cardboard *[1 mark]*
    Reasons: e.g. it's strong, so can withstand the force of other boxes being stacked on top of it without bending. It's good at retaining heat, so keeps the pizza warm. *[Maximum 2 marks, 1 for each correct reason]*.
4 a)   E.g. kraft paper — food packaging / greaseproof paper — baking *[1 mark for type of paper, 1 for correct application]*.
   b)   Any two from: e.g. strength / brightness / colour *[2 marks]*
5   How to grade your answer:
    [No marks] There is no relevant information.
    [1-2 marks] Brief consideration of the positive and negative aspects of each property with regards to packaging. Limited or no conclusion drawn. Points discussed may be limited to only positive OR negative aspects.
    [3-4 marks] Positive AND negative aspects of each property discussed and supported with sensible explanation. Conclusion drawn after considering positive and negatives aspects of each property.
    Here are some points your answer may include:
    Rigidity:
    Packaging needs to be rigid so that it keeps its shape and gives effective protection to what is inside.
    Rigid packaging is more difficult to form, as it is hard to bend/fold it into a 3D shape (e.g. a cardboard box).
    Strength:
    Packaging needs to be strong so it can withstand a fair amount of force before bending and/or breaking.
    Strong packaging is usually heavier/bulkier, which can increase transport costs.

Page 48 — Standard Components

Warm-up
staples, plastic comb, tabs, treasury tags, Velcro® pads, drawing pins

1 a)   E.g. self-seal envelopes/peel and seal envelopes *[1 mark]*.
    The seal is difficult to break without tearing the envelope, so it's obvious if the letter has been tampered with *[1 mark]*.
   b)   e.g. a treasury tag *[1 mark]*
2   Using standard components saves time during manufacture / is more efficient *[1 mark]*. Using standard components means that specialist machinery and extra materials aren't needed, which saves money *[1 mark]*.

Section Four

3 a) Pages are folded in sections *[1 mark]*. Each section is roughened at the fold and glued to the spine *[1 mark]*.

   b) The pages in a thread sewn binding are less likely to come loose than with a perfect binding *[1 mark]*.

   c) comb binding *[1 mark]*

Pages 49-50 — Working with Paper and Board

Warm-up

creasing, cutting, folding, scoring, perforating

1 E.g. a laser cutter *[1 mark]* — it uses a very fine laser beam to burn away parts of the paper *[1 mark]*.

2 a) A 2D plan for making a 3D object, e.g. a box *[1 mark]*.

   b) i) e.g. die cutter *[1 mark]*

      ii) E.g. it cuts out the net from a sheet of material using a sharp blade specially shaped to the outline of the net *[1 mark]*. It also has rounded creasing bars to crease the material along the lines where the material is to be folded *[1 mark]*.

      iii) E.g. because the blade has to be made especially to match the net *[1 mark]*.

   c) E.g. a line of small cuts will be made along the dashed line *[1 mark]*. This line can be torn along easily *[1 mark]*.

3 a) e.g. a circle cutter *[1 mark]*

   b) i) e.g. a guillotine *[1 mark]*

      ii) E.g. it can cut many sheets at a time *[1 mark]* and produces a very straight edge *[1 mark]*.

   c) Name of tool: e.g. a trimming knife *[1 mark]*.
   How to grade your answer:
   [No marks] There is no relevant information.
   [1 mark] There is a brief description of the method, but some stages are left out and the answer contains a number of errors. AND/OR there is a diagram but it lacks detail and clarity.
   [2 marks] There is a detailed description of the method, with stages in the correct order but with some errors. AND/OR there is a well-annotated diagram, but there are some errors.
   [3 marks] There is a clear, accurate and detailed description of the method, including the key stages in the correct order. AND/OR there is a clear, accurate and appropriately annotated diagram showing the method with stages in the correct order.
   Here are some points your answer may include:
   Use a ruler and pencil to accurately mark out the midline of the card, where it needs to be folded.
   Line up a metal ruler along the line, and use it to run the knife along the line.
   Only press lightly with the knife to avoid cutting the paper.
   (Relevant, labelled sketches with annotations showing these points should also be credited.)

   d) E.g. it cuts very precisely *[1 mark]*.

Pages 51-52 — Printing Techniques

Warm-up

newspapers — lithography, flyers — digital printing,
wallpaper — flexography.

1 a) i) e.g. screen printing *[1 mark]*

      ii) E.g. a stencil is put under a fine mesh screen *[1 mark]*. Ink is spread over the top of the screen, and goes through the stencil on to the material underneath *[1 mark]*.

   b) E.g. screen printing is not suitable for this design *[1 mark]* — the design is too complicated to be printed using a screen and stencil *[1 mark]*.

2 a) i) E.g. gravure *[1 mark]*

      ii) E.g. a brass plate that has been etched with the image to be printed *[1 mark]*.

   b) E.g. products printed using lithography are of a lower quality than those produced by other techniques such as gravure *[1 mark]*.

3 a) To print particular colours that cannot be achieved with CMYK *[1 mark]*.

   b) E.g. digital printing has lower set-up costs than other printing techniques *[1 mark]*. The cost of printing per sheet is much higher with digital printing than other techniques, so digital printing is not suitable for larger print runs *[1 mark]*.

4 a) How to grade your answer:
   [No marks] There is no relevant information.
   [1 mark] There is a brief description of the technique, but key stages are left out and the answer contains a number of errors. AND/OR there is a diagram but it lacks detail and clarity.
   [2 marks] There is a description of the technique, but some points are missing or there are some errors. AND/OR there is a diagram with some annotations, but it lacks detail or contains errors.
   [3 marks] There is a detailed description of the technique, with most stages in the correct order but the description may contain small errors or lack some clarity. AND/OR there is an annotated diagram, which is mainly correct but some points are missing.
   [4 marks] There is a clear, accurate and detailed description of the technique, including the key stages in the correct order. AND/OR there is an accurate and appropriately annotated diagram clearly showing the technique.
   Here are some points your answer may include:
   Ultraviolet light is used to transfer an image on to an aluminium printing plate.
   The image area on the plate is then coated with a chemical that attracts oil-based ink but repels water.
   The image area holds ink and the non-image area holds water.
   The image is printed on to a rubber 'blanket' cylinder which squeezes away the water and transfers the ink to the paper.
   (Relevant, labelled sketches with annotations showing these points should also be credited.)

   b) i) e.g. flexible rubber / plastic *[1 mark]*

      ii) Any two from: e.g. flexography is quicker than lithography / flexography printing plates last longer / flexography can be used to print on products that aren't completely smooth *[2 marks]*.

Pages 53-54 — Paper and Board Finishes

Warm-up

Laminating, can't, spot varnishing

1 a) Any two from: e.g. print finishes are used to improve the appearance of a product/make a product look more professional, so people want to buy it / print finishes can protect the product and prevent it from being damaged *[2 marks]*.

   b) E.g. they can be expensive *[1 mark]*.

2 a) The paper or card is placed between two layers of plastic *[1 mark]*. A laminating machine is used to heat the plastic and seal the layers together *[1 mark]*.

   b) E.g. it protects products from being damaged *[1 mark]*, and gives them a shiny or matt finish *[1 mark]*.

3 a) E.g. to give products a glossy or matt finish *[1 mark]*, so they look more exciting/high quality *[1 mark]*.

   b) e.g. magazine/book covers / playing cards / postcards / business cards *[1 mark]*

   c) The varnish is sprayed onto the product *[1 mark]*.
   The varnish is then cured under UV light *[1 mark]*.

4 a) i) It's when metal foil is printed onto certain areas of a product *[1 mark]*.

      ii) E.g. the foil can be used to draw attention to their names *[1 mark]*, and to make the invitations look high quality *[1 mark]*.

      iii) It's when a shaped die is used to leave a raised impression on the surface of paper or board *[1 mark]*.

   b) i) Quote 1 = 180 ÷ 100 = £1.80
      Quote 2 = 340 ÷ 100 = £3.40 *[1 mark for two correct prices]*

      ii) £3.40 − £1.80 = £1.60 *[1 mark]*

The cost of embossing each invitation can be calculated by subtracting the cost per invitation of quote 2 (which includes embossing) from the price per invitation of quote 1 (which includes all features except embossing).

      iii) $((340 - 180) \div 180) \times 100 = 88.9\%$ *[2 marks for an answer of 88.9 — 1 mark for correct working but incorrect final answer]*

To work out the percentage increase you need to divide the difference between the two quotes (the amount that quote 2 is higher than quote 1) by the original number (quote 1) and multiply the result by 100.

Section Five

Section Five — Wood, Metals and Polymers

Pages 55-56 — Uses of Wood, Metals and Polymers

Warm-up

metal, more, less, easier

1 a) E.g. cooking utensils will be exposed to heat during use. Material B will cope with this, but material C may melt when heated due to its low melting point *[1 mark]*.
  b) Material A is hard/tough/strong, which means it can be used for a blade that will cut other materials without breaking *[1 mark]*.
2 a) Log B because it has a lower moisture content *[1 mark]*.
  b) Any two from: e.g. it makes it stronger / it makes it less likely to rot / it makes it less likely to twist *[2 marks]*.
3 a) e.g. urea formaldehyde *[1 mark]*
  b) E.g. it'll stay hard and rigid even if it's heated again *[1 mark]*, making it heat and fire-resistant *[1 mark]*. It's an electrical insulator *[1 mark]*, which is essential in electrical fittings for safety reasons *[1 mark]*.
4 a) Any two from: e.g. it is resistant to moisture *[1 mark]* so is suitable for outdoor use *[1 mark]*. / it's quite tough/flexible/strong *[1 mark]* so can withstand people sitting down on it over and over again *[1 mark]*. / it can be easily moulded *[1 mark]* into shapes that are comfortable to sit on *[1 mark]*.
  b) E.g. the polypropylene seats are used outside, where they will be exposed to UV light from the sun *[1 mark]*. UV light can damage the polypropylene by causing its chemical structure to change *[1 mark]*. This can cause the polypropylene to change colour/fade/lose its strength/become brittle/get a powdery residue on its surface *[1 mark]*. Adding a stabiliser protects the structure of the polypropylene from UV, and prevents these changes from happening *[1 mark]*.

Pages 57-58 — Stock Forms and Standard Components

1 a) sheet *[1 mark]*
  b) rod/tube *[1 mark]*
  c) E.g. it can be very difficult to convert one metal shape to another *[1 mark]*. If there is a wide range of shapes and sizes available it means that manufacturers can buy roughly the right shape to start working with *[1 mark]*.
2 a) E.g. total length of timber required for one frame =
      (300 × 2) + (400 × 2) = 1400 mm
      Length of one standard length in mm =
      1 × 1000 = 1000 mm
      1400 ÷ 1000 = 1.4, so 2 standard lengths are needed.
      [2 marks for correct answer, otherwise 1 mark for correct length of timber required for one frame]
      As you can only buy whole standard lengths of timber, 2 are needed to have enough wood for the frame.
  b) i) mouldings *[1 mark]*
     ii) e.g. skirting boards / door frames *[1 mark]*
  c) sheets *[1 mark]*
3 a) i) e.g. film *[1 mark]*
     ii) e.g. foam *[1 mark]*
  b) e.g. granules / powders *[1 mark]*
  c) 1800 μm = 1800 ÷ 1000 = 1.8 mm *[1 mark]*
      The polymer sheet is suitable as it is thicker than 1.5 mm *[1 mark]*.
      To convert from μm to mm, you just have to divide the thickness in μm by 1000.
4 a) A screw which drills its own threaded holes in hard materials *[1 mark]*.
  b) e.g. metal/plastic sheets *[1 mark]*
  c) E.g.
      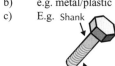
      Diagram showing a bolt with a hexagonal head *[1 mark]*.
      Correctly labelled thread and shank *[1 mark]*.
  d) spanner *[1 mark]*

Page 59 — More Standard Components

1 a) i) e.g. a butt hinge / flush hinge / pivot hinge *[1 mark]*
     ii) any two from: e.g. steel / brass / nylon *[2 marks]*
  b) i) E.g. KD fittings are temporary joints that allow furniture to be assembled quickly and easily *[1 mark]*. This is important for flat-packed furniture as it will need to be self-assembled *[1 mark]*.
     ii) e.g. single blocks / dowels *[1 mark]*
2   How to grade your answer:
    [No marks] There is no relevant information.
    [1 mark] There is a brief description of the method, but key stages are left out and the answer contains a number of errors. AND/OR there is a diagram but it lacks detail and clarity.
    [2 marks] There is a description of the method, but some points are missing or there are some errors. AND/OR there is a diagram with some annotations, but it lacks detail or contains errors.
    [3 marks] There is a detailed description of the method, with most stages in the correct order but the description may contain small errors or lack some clarity. AND/OR there is an annotated diagram, which is mainly correct but some points are missing.
    [4 marks] There is a clear, accurate and detailed description of the method, including the key stages in the correct order. AND/OR there is an accurate and appropriately annotated diagram clearly showing the method.
    Here are some points your answer may include:
    A rivet is a metal peg with a head at one end.
    A hole is drilled through both pieces of metal.
    The rivet is inserted into the hole with a set.
    The head is held against the metal whilst the other end is flattened and shaped into another head using a hammer.
    (Relevant, labelled sketches with annotations showing these points should also be credited.)

Page 60 — Shaping Materials — Hand Tools

1 a) Hand tool: e.g. a coping saw *[1 mark]*.
      Reason: e.g. because it can be used to cut curves in plastic *[1 mark]*.
  b) e.g. a hole saw *[1 mark]*
2 a) e.g. rip saw / tenon saw *[1 mark]*
  b) e.g. so an even pressure can be applied / to give better grip *[1 mark]*
  c) E.g. the bradawl creates a dent *[1 mark]*, which helps you to drill in the right place / stop the drill from slipping *[1 mark]*.
  d) e.g. bench plane *[1 mark]*

Pages 61-62 — Power and Machine Tools

Warm-up

A: router, B: saw bench

1   E.g. a saw bench has a circular blade, whereas a band saw has a blade in a long flexible loop *[1 mark]*. A saw bench can only be used to make straight cuts, whereas a band saw can be used to make straight or curved cuts *[1 mark]*.
2   E.g. a jigsaw *[1 mark]*, because it can be used to cut along the curved outline of the tree *[1 mark]*.
3 a) Any three from: e.g. do a visual check for any loose connections / check for any cuts in insulation along the lead / check the blade or drill bit is attached correctly / check the blade or drill bit is attached tightly / use a residual current device/RCD / wear a mask if the tool produces dust / fit an extraction hose if the tool produces dust / wear safety glasses / make sure clothing doesn't get caught / clamp the work firmly so it doesn't move / make sure you know where the stop button is before you start / make sure the tool has stopped moving before you put it down *[3 marks]*.
  b) E.g. machine tools are often more accurate than power tools / machine tools are better suited to bigger tasks than power tools *[1 mark]*.
4 a) i) e.g. a hand-held router *[1 mark]*
     ii) e.g. use a fence *[1 mark]*
  b) e.g. a pillar drill *[1 mark]*

Answers

Section Five

c)   e.g. a planer *[1 mark]*

5 a)   The machine spins a disc of abrasive paper, which material is pushed against to be sanded down *[1 mark]*.

b)   E.g. it would use a different type of abrasive paper *[1 mark]*.

c)   e.g. a dust extractor *[1 mark]*

Pages 63-64 — Shaping Techniques

Warm-up

True, false

1 a)   E.g. line bender / strip heater *[1 mark]*

b)   E.g. the sheet of plastic is positioned on top of the line bender *[1 mark]* so that the heating element is directly below the line to be bent *[1 mark]*. This softens the plastic so it can be bent into shape *[1 mark]*.

2   How to grade your answer:

[No marks] There is no relevant information.

[1 mark] There is a brief description of the process, but key stages are left out and the answer contains a number of errors. AND/OR there is a diagram but it lacks detail and clarity.

[2 marks] There is a description of the process, but some points are missing or there are some errors. AND/OR there is a diagram with some annotations, but it lacks detail or contains errors.

[3 marks] There is a detailed description of the process, with most stages in the correct order but the description may contain small errors or lack some clarity. AND/OR there is an annotated diagram, which is mainly correct but some points are missing.

[4 marks] There is a clear, accurate and detailed description of the process, including the key stages in the correct order. AND/OR there is an accurate and appropriately annotated diagram clearly showing the process.

Here are some points your answer may include:

The metal is melted.

It is then poured into a mould/die, which is in the shape of the model car's body.

The metal is left to cool and solidify.

The body of the model car can be removed from the mould and trimmed to remove any excess material.

(Relevant, labelled sketches with annotations showing these points should also be credited.)

3   Ideas can be designed on a computer using computer aided design (CAD) software packages *[1 mark]*. A 3D printer uses this to convert the design into a 3D model, by printing layers of molten plastic/powder/wax until the full 3D shape has been formed *[1 mark]*.

4 a)   How to grade your answer:

[No marks] There is no relevant information.

[1 mark] There is a brief description of the process, but key stages are left out and the answer contains a number of errors. AND/OR there is a diagram but it lacks detail and clarity.

[2 marks] There is a description of the process, but some points are missing or there are some errors. AND/OR there is a diagram with some annotations, but it lacks detail or contains errors.

[3 marks] There is a detailed description of the process, with most stages in the correct order but the description may contain small errors or lack some clarity. AND/OR there is an annotated diagram, which is mainly correct but some points are missing.

[4 marks] There is a clear, accurate and detailed description of the process, including the key stages in the correct order. AND/OR there is an accurate and appropriately annotated diagram clearly showing the process.

Here are some points your answer may include:

Thin strips of wood are glued together.

The glued strips of wood are placed into a jig.

The jig holds the wood in a bent position until the glue has dried.

The strips of wood can then be taken out of the jig and stay bent, so can be used for rockers.

(Relevant, labelled sketches with annotations showing these points should also be credited.)

b) i)   e.g. a lathe/wood lathe *[1 mark]*

ii)   E.g. the lathe holds the wood and rotates it *[1 mark]*. A tool/bit can then be pressed into the wood to cut it as it rotates *[1 mark]*.

Pages 65-67 — Moulding and Joining

1 a)   e.g. polyvinyl acetate glue/PVA glue *[1 mark]*

b)   Advantage: e.g. it sets quickly *[1 mark]*

Disadvantage: e.g. it isn't cheap *[1 mark]*

2   How to grade your answer:

[No marks] There is no relevant information.

[1 mark] There is a brief description of the process, but key stages are left out and the answer contains a number of errors. AND/OR there is a diagram but it lacks detail and clarity.

[2 marks] There is a description of the process, but some points are missing or there are some errors. AND/OR there is a diagram with some annotations, but it lacks detail or contains errors.

[3 marks] There is a detailed description of the process, with most stages in the correct order but the description may contain small errors or lack some clarity. AND/OR there is an annotated diagram, which is mainly correct but some points are missing.

[4 marks] There is a clear, accurate and detailed description of the process, including the key stages in the correct order. AND/OR there is an accurate and appropriately annotated diagram clearly showing the process.

Here are some points your answer may include:

Plastic granules are fed into the hopper/machine.

The granules are heated in a chamber in the machine until they melt.

The molten plastic is then forced into a closed mould/die under pressure.

The plastic sets and the mould is removed.

(Relevant, labelled sketches with annotations showing these points should also be credited.)

3 a)   Solder is heated up and melted using a soldering iron/blow torch *[1 mark]*. The molten solder flows between the two metals and cools and solidifies to form the joint *[1 mark]*.

b) i)   e.g. brass spelter *[1 mark]*

ii)   E.g. joints formed using brazing are stronger than soldered joints *[1 mark]*.

c)   E.g. the process melts the edges of the joint so that the plastic flows together *[1 mark]*. You can melt the edges using a hot gas welding gun/using lasers/by vibrating one side of the joint against the other side of the joint at high speed/using solvents *[1 mark]*. Thermoplastic welding rods can be used to melt thermoplastic into the join *[1 mark]*.

4   Moulding process: Plastic bottle — blow moulding / Plastic guttering — extrusion *[1 mark]*

Plastic bottles are hollow, so blow moulding is a suitable choice. Plastic guttering is a long continuous strip with the same cross-section throughout, so extrusion is a suitable moulding process to use.

How to grade your answer:

[No marks] There is no relevant information.

[1 mark] There is a brief description of the process, but key stages are left out and the answer contains a number of errors. AND/OR there is a diagram but it lacks detail and clarity.

[2 marks] There is a description of the process, but some points are missing or there are some errors. AND/OR there is a diagram with some annotations, but it lacks detail or contains errors.

[3 marks] There is a detailed description of the process, with most stages in the correct order but the description may contain small errors or lack some clarity. AND/OR there is an annotated diagram, which is mainly correct but some points are missing.

[4 marks] There is a clear, accurate and detailed description of the process, including the key stages in the correct order. AND/OR there is an accurate and appropriately annotated diagram clearly showing the process.

Here are some points your answer may include:

Blow moulding:

This process starts with a tube of softened plastic.

Section Six

The plastic is inserted into a solid mould.

Air is injected into the tube of plastic, forcing the plastic to expand.

The plastic takes the shape of the inside of the mould.

The mould is opened to remove the plastic bottle.

Extrusion:

The plastic is heated in a chamber in the machine until it melts.

The liquid plastic is then forced through a mould/die under pressure.

This produces a long continuous strip of plastic/guttering.

The guttering will have the same cross-section as the shape of the exit hole.

(Relevant, labelled sketches with annotations showing these points should also be credited.)

5 a) Method: e.g. drape forming *[1 mark]*

b) How to grade your answer:

[No marks] There is no relevant information.

[1 mark] There is a brief description of the method, but some stages are left out and the answer contains a number of errors. AND/OR there is a diagram but it lacks detail and clarity.

[2 marks] There is a detailed description of the method, with stages in the correct order but with some errors. AND/OR there is a well-annotated diagram, but there are some errors.

[3 marks] There is a clear, accurate and detailed description of the method, including the key stages in the correct order. AND/OR there is a clear, accurate and appropriately annotated diagram showing the method with stages in the correct order.

Here are some points your answer may include:

(Relevant, labelled sketches with annotations showing these points should also be credited.)

A sheet of thermoforming plastic is heated until it softens.

The softened plastic is placed onto a mould in the curved shape of the lamp shade.

The plastic is left to cool on the mould.

When removed from the mould, the plastic will be the desired shape.

c) E.g. the decorative plastic pieces could be attached to the shade using glue, e.g. solvent cement *[1 mark]*.

Pages 68-69 — Treatments and Finishes

1 a) E.g. reacting/coming into contact with both oxygen and water *[1 mark]*.

b) galvanising/galvanisation *[1 mark]*

c) The zinc layer acts as a barrier, stopping the water and oxygen from coming into contact with the steel *[1 mark]*.

If the layer of zinc is scratched to expose steel, the zinc will react first with the oxygen/water rather than steel which prevents rust forming *[1 mark]*.

2 a) A sanding sealer should be applied to the oak *[1 mark]*. The oak should then be sanded in the direction of the grain using abrasive paper *[1 mark]*.

b) E.g. oak grain markings are attractive. They can be seen beneath a varnish but not beneath paint *[1 mark]*.

c) e.g. polyurethane varnish *[1 mark]*, because it is very hard-wearing *[1 mark]*

3 a) e.g. to change its colour *[1 mark]*.

b) Any two from: e.g. primer fills the grain of the timber to give the paint on top a smooth finish / the primer helps to seal the timber, so the paint won't soak in and need re-applying / primer helps the paint stick better to the timber *[2 marks]*.

c) e.g. undercoat *[1 mark]*

d) E.g. tanalised® wood is protected from insect attacks/decay if the paint layer is damaged *[1 mark]*.

4 a) Metals need to be smoothed by filing and rubbing with abrasive paper and wet and dry paper *[1 mark]*. Grease then needs to be removed from the metals surface *[1 mark]*.

b) How to grade your answer:

[No marks] There is no relevant information.

[1 mark] There is a brief description of the method, but key stages are left out and the answer contains a number of errors. AND/OR there is a diagram but it lacks detail and clarity.

[2 marks] There is a description of the method, but some points are missing or there are some errors. AND/OR there is a diagram with some annotations, but it lacks detail or contains errors.

[3 marks] There is a detailed description of the method, with most stages in the correct order but the description may contain small errors or lack some clarity. AND/OR there is an annotated diagram, which is mainly correct but some points are missing.

[4 marks] There is a clear, accurate and detailed description of the method, including the key stages in the correct order. AND/OR there is an accurate and appropriately annotated diagram clearly showing the method.

Here are some points your answer may include:

Plastic powder is sprayed onto the metal using an electrostatic gun.

The spray gun gives the powder an electrical charge.

The particles have the same charge so they repel each other to form a fine, even spray.

The metal to be coated is given the opposite charge to the gun so it attracts the fine spray.

After spraying, the object is heated in an oven.

The powder undergoes a chemical change in the oven and sets hard.

(Relevant, labelled sketches with annotations showing these points should also be credited.)

c) E.g. the method gives an even coat / there's hardly any waste from the method *[1 mark]*.

Section Six — Textiles

Pages 70-71 — Fabrics and Their Properties

Warm-up

Flame retardance, stain protection, water resistance

1 Any two from: e.g. they're warm/soft to walk on / they're resistant to fading *[2 marks]*

2 a) E.g. water-resistant treatment *[1 mark]* — it would stop rain from passing through the coat *[1 mark]*.

b) E.g. stain-resistant treatment *[1 mark]* — it would stop the carpet from becoming stained if food were dropped onto it *[1 mark]*.

3 E.g. polyester is strong / resistant to abrasion *[1 mark]*, so the T-shirt won't easily be damaged during sports *[1 mark]*. Polyester dries very quickly *[1 mark]*, so is suitable for outdoor use / when sweating *[1 mark]*.

4 a) It makes a fabric less likely to catch fire *[1 mark]*.

b) E.g. welders work with flames and hot metal *[1 mark]*.

c) e.g. racing drivers' overalls / children's night clothes *[1 mark]*

d) E.g. flame retardant treatments can be washed out / can make a fabric slightly stiffer *[1 mark]*.

5 a) lamination *[1 mark]*

b) E.g. they can add strength to the fabric *[1 mark]* and protect the delicate waterproof membrane *[1 mark]*.

c) E.g. water-resistant finishes let water through if the fabric becomes saturated with water *[1 mark]*.

Pages 72-73 — Standard Components and Tools

1 E.g. to flatten seams *[1 mark]* / to apply designs from transfers onto fabric *[1 mark]* / to fix designs done with fabric crayons permanently onto a fabric *[1 mark]*.

2 a) e.g. tailor's chalk *[1 mark]* and pattern masters *[1 mark]*

b) i) Dressmaking scissors have very long blades, whereas embroidery scissors have short blades *[1 mark]*.

ii) Dressmaking scissors are used to neatly cut through fabric *[1 mark]*, whereas embroidery scissors are used for more delicate cutting, e.g. snipping threads *[1 mark]*.

c) E.g. scissors might accidentally cut the fabric when cutting a seam, whereas seam rippers wouldn't *[1 mark]*.

3 a) One half of the Velcro® has rough nylon hooks which attach to the soft loops on the other half *[1 mark]*.

b) How to grade your answer:

[No marks] There is no relevant information.

[1-2 marks] Brief consideration of the positive and negative aspects of using Velcro® in the apron. Limited or no conclusion

Section Six

drawn. Points discussed may be limited to only positive OR negative aspects.

[3-4 marks] Positive AND negative aspects of Velcro® discussed and supported with sensible explanations. Conclusion drawn after considering positive and negatives aspects of Velcro®. Here are some points your answer may include:

Velcro® isn't a choking hazard so is safe for children.

Velcro® can be machine washed so the apron can be cleaned regularly.

Velcro® is hard-wearing so will withstand child's play.

The hooks will collect fibres from clothes and become less effective/sticky over time.

Velcro® isn't very attractive so doesn't add to the decoration of the apron.

This question is asking you to evaluate the Velcro® fastening, so you need to give both advantages and disadvantages of Velcro®, and draw a conclusion. Your points should also be specific to the product in the question — in this case, you should focus on how suitable the product is for children.

4 a) Fabric A: total cost = 5.50 × 1.70 = £9.35
Fabric B: total cost = 7.40 × 1.55 = £11.47
[1 mark for two correct total costs]

b) i) Total cost = 6.20 × 1.90 = £11.78 *[1 mark]*

ii) Area of fabric C required for the original design
= 1.50 × 1.55 = 2.325 m² *[1 mark]*
Area of fabric C required for the revised design
= 1.50 × 1.90 = 2.85 m² *[1 mark]*

The width of the fabric is given in cm so this needs to be converted to metres in these calculations, i.e. 155 cm ÷ 100 = 1.55 m.

Difference in area = 2.85 − 2.325 = 0.525 m²
= 0.53 m² (to 2 decimal places) *[1 mark]*

c) E.g. press studs can be opened and closed quicker than buttons *[1 mark]*.

Pages 74-77 — Joining and Shaping Fabrics

Warm-up

False, true, false

1 a) To join the edges of fabric pieces together securely *[1 mark]*.

b) How to grade your answer:
[No marks] There is no relevant information.
[1 mark] There is a brief description of the method, but key stages are left out and the answer contains a number of errors. AND/OR there is a diagram but it lacks detail and clarity.
[2 marks] There is a description of the method, but some points are missing or there are some errors. AND/OR there is a diagram with some annotations, but it lacks detail or contains errors.
[3 marks] There is a detailed description of the method, with most stages in the correct order but the description may contain small errors or lack some clarity. AND/OR there is an annotated diagram, which is mainly correct but some points are missing.
[4 marks] There is a clear, accurate and detailed description of the method, including the key stages in the correct order. AND/OR there is an accurate and appropriately annotated diagram clearly showing the method.
Here are some points your answer may include:
Arrange two pieces of fabric so their outward facing sides are touching.
Using pins, a needle and some thread, pin and tack the pieces of fabric to hold them in place.
Use a needle and thread/a sewing machine to stitch about 1.5 cm in from the edge of the fabric.
Reverse back over the seam.
Finish the seam edges.
Open out the seam and iron it so it lies flat.
(Relevant, labelled sketches with annotations showing these points should also be credited.)

c) E.g. plain seams aren't very strong *[1 mark]*, so they aren't very suitable for use in a rugby shirt where the seams are likely to be put under a lot of strain *[1 mark]*.

d) i) A french seam *[1 mark]* because there are no rough edges to irritate delicate skin *[1 mark]*.

ii) A flat felled seam *[1 mark]* because it's strong / stops edges from fraying *[1 mark]*.

2   An overlocker will sew, trim and neaten the seams all at once *[1 mark]*. This is more efficient than using a sewing machine, because neatening the edges will have to be done separately *[1 mark]*.

3 a) Quilting is the process of sewing wadding between two layers of fabric *[1 mark]*. The fabric layers are then stitched together in straight lines or in a pattern *[1 mark]*.

b) The wadding keeps the wearer warm/traps warm air between the layers of fabric *[1 mark]*.

4 a) i) E.g. when doing a lot of sewing *[1 mark]* because using a machine is much faster than hand-sewing *[1 mark]*.

ii) E.g. for small tasks like embroidery or darning *[1 mark]* because hand-sewing is more precise *[1 mark]*.

b) E.g. to check that the thread tension / stitch length / stitch type is correct *[1 mark]*.

5 a) How to grade your answer:
[No marks] There is no relevant information.
[1 mark] There is a brief description of the method, but some stages are left out and the answer contains a number of errors. AND/OR there is a diagram but it lacks detail and clarity.
[2 marks] There is a detailed description of the method, with stages in the correct order but with some errors. AND/OR there is a well-annotated diagram, but there are some errors.
[3 marks] There is a clear, accurate and detailed description of the method, including the key stages in the correct order. AND/OR there is a clear, accurate and appropriately annotated diagram showing the method with stages in the correct order.
Here are some points your answer may include:
Piping is made from a strip of material that has folded fabric/ cord sewn inside.
Line up the pieces of fabric on either side of the piping's seam allowance.
Lay the pieces of fabric face down onto the piping's seam allowance.
Sew a line of stitching over the fabric pieces to attach them to the piping.
Unfold the fabric and iron the underside of the seam.
(Relevant, labelled sketches with annotations showing these points should also be credited.)

b) E.g. to add decoration to a product *[1 mark]*, to add strength to a product *[1 mark]*.

6 a) To stop the fabrics from slipping whilst they are being sewn together *[1 mark]*.

b) How to grade your answer:
[No marks] There is no relevant information.
[1 mark] There is a brief description of the process, but some stages are left out and the answer contains a number of errors. AND/OR there is a diagram but it lacks detail and clarity.
[2 marks] There is a detailed description of the process, with stages in the correct order but with some errors. AND/OR there is a well-annotated diagram, but there are some errors.
[3 marks] There is a clear, accurate and detailed description of the process, including the key stages in the correct order. AND/OR there is a clear, accurate and appropriately annotated diagram showing the process with stages in the correct order.
Here are some points your answer may include:
The fabrics are pinned by putting pins at right angles to the edge of the fabric, along the line that is to be sewn.
The fabrics can then be tacked by hand sewing long running stitches about 1 cm in length along the fabrics.
The thread used to tack the fabrics should be a different colour to the fabric so it can be easily seen.
(Relevant, labelled sketches with annotations showing these points should also be credited.)

c) E.g. paperclips / bulldog clips can be used to temporarily hold the fabrics together *[1 mark]*.

7 a) CAD software can be used to draw a design which can be transferred to a CAM embroidery machine *[1 mark]*. This machine follows the design to produce the embroidery *[1 mark]*.

Section Seven

b) E.g. a CAM embroidery machine will embroider the fabric quicker / more accurately than by hand *[1 mark]*.

8 a) How to grade your answer:
[No marks] There is no relevant information.
[1 mark] There is a brief description of the process, but key stages are left out and the answer contains a number of errors. AND/OR there is a diagram but it lacks detail and clarity.
[2 marks] There is a description of the process, but some points are missing or there are some errors. AND/OR there is a diagram with some annotations, but it lacks detail or contains errors.
[3 marks] There is a detailed description of the process, with most stages in the correct order but the description may contain small errors or lack some clarity. AND/OR there is an annotated diagram, which is mainly correct but some points are missing.
[4 marks] There is a clear, accurate and detailed description of the process, including the key stages in the correct order. AND/OR there is an accurate and appropriately annotated diagram clearly showing the process.
Here are some points your answer may include:
Folds are made in the fabric of the skirt.
The folds are pinned into position.
The folds are stitched across their top to permanently keep them in position.
The folds are pressed (using an iron) to give them sharp creases.
(Relevant, labelled sketches with annotations showing these points should also be credited.)

b) Name: e.g. gathering *[1 mark]*.
Description: e.g. two parallel rows of stitches are sewn in the seam allowance *[1 mark]*. The threads are then pulled and the fabric eased along until it is drawn to the right size *[1 mark]*. The gathering is then fixed in place by knotting the threads at the end of the gather *[1 mark]*.

Pages 78-79 — Dyeing

1 a) To change the colour/appearance of a fabric *[1 mark]*.
b) e.g. onions / beetroot / tea / raspberries / flowers *[1 mark]*
c) E.g. because some chemical dyes are toxic/can be harmful to people and the environment *[1 mark]*.

2 a) E.g. a large amount of fabric can be dyed at once / fabric can be dyed quickly *[1 mark]*.
b) E.g. a resist can be used to add designs to a fabric / it produces unique products *[1 mark]*.

3 E.g. some dyes become insoluble in water when oxidised *[1 mark]*. This means that they become colour-fast/won't dissolve and come out in the wash *[1 mark]*.

4 a) E.g. cotton / wool / silk *[1 mark]*, because they are absorbent *[1 mark]*.
b) Because they have an uneven colour and won't dye evenly unless they're bleached *[1 mark]*.

5 a) E.g. a batch of fabric is mounted on two rollers *[1 mark]* and is passed back and forth through the dye *[1 mark]*. It is then put in a separate machine to fix the dye and wash any excess dye off *[1 mark]*.
b) E.g. it allows manufacturers to respond quickly to orders for a specific colour of fabric *[1 mark]*.

6 a) A resist is applied in a pattern before dyeing and prevents the dye from reaching the fabric *[1 mark]*.
b) i) e.g. batik *[1 mark]*
ii) E.g. hot wax is applied with a brush or tjanting to create a pattern *[1 mark]*. When the wax is dry, the dye is painted on / the fabric is immersed in a dye bath *[1 mark]*. Then the wax is ironed off to reveal the pattern *[1 mark]*.
c) i) E.g. tie-dyeing *[1 mark]*. String / rubber bands are used as a resist *[1 mark]*.
ii) Any two from: e.g. the outcome is unpredictable / the pattern cannot be repeated exactly / detailed patterns can't be made / it's time-consuming for large areas of fabric *[2 marks]*.

Pages 80-81 — Printing

1 dyes *[1 mark]*, paints *[1 mark]*

2 a) e.g. a squeegee *[1 mark]*, a screen *[1 mark]*
b) How to grade your answer:
[No marks] There is no relevant information.
[1 mark] There is a brief description of the process, but key stages are left out and the answer contains a number of errors. AND/OR there is a diagram but it lacks detail and clarity.
[2 marks] There is a description of the process, but some points are missing or there are some errors. AND/OR there is a diagram with some annotations, but it lacks detail or contains errors.
[3 marks] There is a detailed description of the process, with most stages in the correct order but the description may contain small errors or lack some clarity. AND/OR there is an annotated diagram, which is mainly correct but some points are missing.
[4 marks] There is a clear, accurate and detailed description of the process, including the key stages in the correct order. AND/OR there is an accurate and appropriately annotated diagram clearly showing the process.
Here are some points your answer may include:
A stencil of the design is cut from card or acetate and placed on top of the fabric / parts of a screen are blocked off to create the design.
The screen is placed on top of the stencil/fabric.
Printing ink is poured onto the screen, and a squeegee is pressed down and drawn across the screen.
This forces the ink through the mesh, and the holes in the stencil.
The screen is lifted up and the design is left on the fabric.
(Relevant, labelled sketches with annotations showing these points should also be credited.)
c) Any two from: e.g. a long length of fabric is mounted onto a conveyor belt, which moves it under the screens / Several screens, each with their own colour of ink, are used to print different colours onto the fabric / Metal rods, moving backwards and forwards across the screen, are used as squeegees *[2 marks]*.
d) E.g. rotary screen printing is faster *[1 mark]*.

3 a) How to grade your answer:
[No marks] There is no relevant information.
[1 mark] There is a brief description of the method, but key stages are left out and the answer contains a number of errors. AND/OR there is a diagram but it lacks detail and clarity.
[2 marks] There is a description of the method, but some points are missing or there are some errors. AND/OR there is a diagram with some annotations, but it lacks detail or contains errors.
[3 marks] There is a detailed description of the method, with most stages in the correct order but the description may contain small errors or lack some clarity. AND/OR there is an annotated diagram, which is mainly correct but some points are missing.
[4 marks] There is a clear, accurate and detailed description of the method, including the key stages in the correct order. AND/OR there is an accurate and appropriately annotated diagram clearly showing the method.
Here are some points your answer may include:
The printing block has a raised design.
The design is star-shaped.
Printing ink is applied to the raised surface of the block.
The block is pressed down onto the fabric to transfer the star design to the fabric.
(Relevant, labelled sketches with annotations showing these points should also be credited.)
b) Any two from, e.g. different colours (for the different stars) can be printed using the same printing block / the design can be easily repeated / the block won't wear out easily *[2 marks]*.
c) E.g. (flat-bed) screen printing *[1 mark]*.

Section Seven — Electronic and Mechanical Systems

Pages 82-83 — Properties of Components in Systems

1 a) A material that responds to being exposed to light *[1 mark]*.
b) UV/ultraviolet light *[1 mark]*

Answers

Section Seven

2   E.g. plastic / stainless steel *[1 mark]* because this material is resistant to corrosion *[1 mark]*.
Exposure to water causes many materials to corrode.

3 a)   The current and voltage values that an electronic component is designed to work at *[1 mark]*.

    b)   E.g. the bulb could heat up and be damaged *[1 mark]*.

4 a)   an electric current *[1 mark]*

    b)   Anodisation thickens the layer of aluminium oxide on the pan *[1 mark]*, making the surface harder so that it doesn't scratch as easily *[1 mark]*.

5 a)   E.g. a toaster / kettle / electric oven *[1 mark]*.

    b)   E.g. a high melting point *[1 mark]*, so it can become hot without melting *[1 mark]* / corrosion-resistant *[1 mark]*, so it doesn't corrode in air/water *[1 mark]*.

6 a)   If the car is involved in an accident, these properties will help the car body absorb the impact of the crash *[1 mark]*, protecting the passengers *[1 mark]*.

    b)   E.g. it improves performance / it improves acceleration / it improves fuel economy *[1 mark]*.

Pages 84-85 — Standard Components in Systems

Warm-up
E12 series — A set of fixed resistors.
Programmable intelligent computer (PIC) — A type of programmable microcontroller.
Integrated circuit (IC) — A tiny circuit contained within a single component.

1 a)   The casing holds/protects the IC *[1 mark]*. The pins connect the IC to the rest of the circuit/PCB *[1 mark]*.

    b)   The pins can be pushed through holes in the PCB and soldered on the other side *[1 mark]*.
       The pins can be plugged into an IC socket *[1 mark]*.

2   PICs with flash memory can be reprogrammed so they can be used again and again, whereas OTP microcontrollers can only be programmed once *[1 mark]*.

3 a)   They reduce the current flowing round a circuit *[1 mark]*.

    b)   10% of 56 ohms = 5.6 ohms *[1 mark]*
       lower limit of the range = 56 − 5.6 = 50.4 ohms *[1 mark]*
       upper limit of the range = 56 + 5.6 = 61.6 ohms *[1 mark]*

    c)   blue, grey, orange *[1 mark]*
The first two bands give the first two digits of the resistance value so you just need to look up their numbers in the table to see what colours they represent (i.e. blue, grey). Band 3 gives the number of zeros that comes after this (3 in this example), so this band is orange.

4 a)   Any two from: e.g. width / number of teeth / tooth shape *[2 marks]*.

    b) i)   Compression springs *[1 mark]* and extension springs *[1 mark]*.

      ii)   Compression springs resist compression, whereas extension springs resist extension *[1 mark]*.

Page 86 — Cutting, Drilling and Soldering

Warm-up

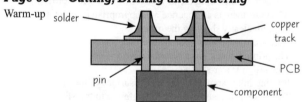

1   It acts as an electrical connection between the component's pins and the copper tracks on the PCB *[1 mark]*.

2   Name: flow/wave soldering *[1 mark]*
    How to grade your answer:
    [No marks] There is no relevant information.
    [1 mark] There is a brief description of the method, but key stages are left out and the answer contains a number of errors. AND/OR there is a diagram but it lacks detail and clarity.
    [2 marks] There is a description of the method, but some points are missing or there are some errors. AND/OR there is a diagram with some annotations, but it lacks detail or contains errors.
    [3 marks] There is a detailed description of the method, with

most stages in the correct order but the description may contain small errors or lack some clarity. AND/OR there is an annotated diagram, which is mainly correct but some points are missing.
[4 marks] There is a clear, accurate and detailed description of the method, including the key stages in the correct order. AND/OR there is an accurate and appropriately annotated diagram clearly showing the method.
Here are some points your answer may include:
Components are placed on the board.
Components are sometimes glued in place.
The board is passed over a pan of molten solder.
A 'wave'/upwelling of solder is produced by a pump.
The wave produced is at the right height to just touch the base of the board as it is passed over the pan, soldering the components in place.
(Relevant, labelled sketches with annotations showing these points should also be credited.)

Pages 87-88 — PCB Production and Surface Treatments

Warm-up
Dipping, painting and spraying should be circled.

1 a)   It reduces friction / it allows surfaces to slip past each other easily *[1 mark]*.

    b)   E.g. it allows the system to operate with a higher efficiency *[1 mark]* and reduces the rate at which interlocking parts are worn down / it reduces the chance of moving parts being damaged *[1 mark]*.

2 a)   It is the process of placing components onto a PCB in the correct position and orientation *[1 mark]*.

    b)   Advantage: e.g. pick and place CAM machines are quicker / more precise / more consistent than assembling PCBs manually *[1 mark]*.
       Disadvantage: e.g. pick and place CAM machines have to be programmed before they can be used, which can be a lengthy process / often can't be used for components with pins that need to be pushed through holes in the PCB *[1 mark]*.

3 a) i)   polymers/plastic *[1 mark]*

      ii)   E.g. it acts as a protective barrier / it helps to decrease corrosion/ increase the durability of the board *[1 mark]*.

    b)   E.g. a UV light can be used to check if there is a good coverage of lacquer on the boards *[1 mark]*, as parts that have not got a coat of lacquer won't glow under UV light *[1 mark]*.

4   How to grade your answer:
    [No marks] There is no relevant information.
    [1 mark] There is a brief description of the process, but key stages are left out and the answer contains a number of errors. AND/OR there is a diagram but it lacks detail and clarity.
    [2 marks] There is a description of the process, but some points are missing or there are some errors. AND/OR there is a diagram with some annotations, but it lacks detail or contains errors.
    [3 marks] There is a detailed description of the process, with most stages in the correct order but the description may contain small errors or lack some clarity. AND/OR there is an annotated diagram, which is mainly correct but some points are missing.
    [4 marks] There is a clear, accurate and detailed description of the process, including the key stages in the correct order. AND/OR there is an accurate and appropriately annotated diagram clearly showing the process.
Here are some points your answer may include:
The layout of the copper tracks is designed using CAD software and printed onto a transparent sheet (e.g. acetate) to form a mask.
The mask is placed on top of the blank PCB and exposed to UV light.
The UV can shine through areas of the mask that are transparent to modify the photosensitive layer underneath.
Where the mask is opaque, the photosensitive material is shielded so is not modified.
The board is then exposed to a developer solution/chemical.

Section Eight

This dissolves the parts of the photosensitive layer that were modified by the UV, exposing the copper beneath.

Next, the board is exposed to an etching solution/chemical, which dissolves any exposed copper on the board, leaving behind the custom copper tracks (which are still protected by the unmodified photosensitive material above).

The remaining photosensitive material is stripped off, exposing the custom copper tracks.

(Relevant, labelled sketches with annotations showing these points should also be credited.)

Section Eight — Designing and Making

Page 89 — Looking at the Work of Designers

Warm-up

Alexander McQueen — Fashion, Gerrit Rietveld — Architecture, Alec Issigonis — Cars, Raymond Templier — Jewellery, Harry Beck — London Underground map, William Morris — Wallpaper, furniture and furnishings

1   How to grade your answer:

[No marks] There is no relevant information.

[1 mark] There is a brief description of the work of one of the named companies. The answer may contain major errors and lack relevant detail.

[2 marks] There is a description of the work of one of the named companies. Some key facts about the company's work are covered but the answer lacks the detail needed to give a clear understanding. Some minor errors may be present.

[3 marks] There is a clear description of the work of one of the named companies. The answer doesn't contain any errors and gives enough key facts to provide an accurate impression of the work of the company.

For this question you must talk about the work of one of the companies listed in the question. There's a huge variety of things that you could say to answer this question, so we've just given advice on how marks would be awarded rather than any specific points to include.

2   How to grade your answer:

[No marks] There is no relevant information.

[1 to 2 marks] There is a brief comparison of the work of two named designers. Discussion of differences and/or similarities between the work of the two designers is vague and the answer contains major errors. Key points about the work of the two designers are missing.

[3 to 4 marks] There is some comparison of the work of the two named designers. Similarities and/or differences given are limited and errors are present.

[5 to 6 marks] There is a good attempt to compare the work of the two named designers. Similarities and differences are discussed. The answer may feature examples to help describe the work of each designer. The answer may lack clarity or contain some minor errors.

[7 to 8 marks] There is a clear, detailed and accurate comparison of the work of the two named designers. Similarities and differences between the work of the designers are discussed thoroughly using examples. There are few, if any, errors in the answer.

This is a big mark question. To get high marks you need to talk about the styles of the designers you've chosen and then compare these. Using examples is a good way to break into the higher marks — this lets you talk about specifics rather than relying on vaguer statements about the sort of work each designer is known for. There's a huge variety of things that you could say to answer this question, so we've just given advice on how marks would be awarded rather than any specific points to include.

Pages 90-91 — Understanding User Needs

1   Any two from: e.g. it would mean that the racket handle was the right length for people's hands / it would mean the overall length of the racket was right so it doesn't hit the floor when swung / it would mean the grip would be the right thickness so it's comfortable to use *[2 marks]*.

2 a)   Group 1: e.g. wheelchair users *[1 mark]*

Reason: e.g. the screen and buttons may be too high for them to use *[1 mark]*.

Group 2: e.g. blind or sight impaired people *[1 mark]*

Reason: they may have difficulty using the buttons or reading the screen *[1 mark]*.

   b)   Group 1 (e.g. wheelchair users): e.g. the machine could be lowered *[1 mark]*.

Group 2 (e.g. sight impaired people): e.g. it could be designed with larger buttons / Braille marks / bigger screen *[1 mark]*.

3 a)   E.g. hand width / finger length *[1 mark]*

   b)   E.g. they could experience long-term health effects/hand strain *[1 mark]*.

4   E.g. children's shoes are often designed to be easy to fasten (e.g. use Velcro®) compared to adult's shoes (e.g. which often use laces) *[1 mark]* because children may find it difficult to manipulate fastenings/laces *[1 mark]*.

5 a)   Any two from: e.g. width of head / distance between ear and mouth / vertical distance between the ear and the top of the head *[2 marks]*

   b)   E.g. manufacturers often make products so that they fit 90% of the target users, using the 5th and 95th percentiles as cut offs *[1 mark]*. A person in the 97th percentile for head size will have head dimensions larger than the range catered for by the headset, so it won't fit their head *[1 mark]*.

6   E.g. the size of the seat is similar to the dimension given in the anthropometric data *[1 mark]*. However the chair legs are 30 mm shorter than the knee to foot length given in the data *[1 mark]*. Also, the chair back height is 90 mm shorter than the waist to back length given in the data *[1 mark]*.

In conclusion, the chair is quite well matched to an average 18-40 year old British male, but the legs could be made 500 mm in length and the chair back 690 mm in height to make it more comfortable to sit on *[1 mark]*.

Pages 92-93 — Design Briefs and Specifications

1 a)   E.g. design a storage system with enough compartments to hold all the plumber's tools so that they don't get mixed up *[1 mark]*.

   b)   E.g. design a small toy/game suitable for children to use on a long journey that will hold their attention *[1 mark]*.

2 a)   E.g. the points are too vague / don't provide specific information / are not quantified *[1 mark]*.

   b)   Point 1 — the rack should hold at least 35 CDs *[1 mark]*, as this is the average number of CDs that people own based on the market research findings *[1 mark]*.

Point 2 — the rack should be silver coloured *[1 mark]*, as this is the most popular choice of colour based on the market research findings *[1 mark]*.

3 a) i)   Any two from: e.g. to check people actually want the product / to find out what people in the target market like or dislike about similar existing products *[2 marks]*.

     ii)   Product analysis *[1 mark]* — it involves examining/disassembling a current product *[1 mark]*.

   b) i)   Any two from: e.g. mice have increased in popularity / hamsters have decreased in popularity / the popularity of guinea pigs has remained roughly constant / hamsters are currently more popular than mice/guinea pigs / mice are currently more popular than guinea pigs *[2 marks]*.

     ii)   E.g. change "all year round" to "in the summer"/"when it's warm enough" *[1 mark]*. 98% of owners who do keep their mice outdoors only do so in summer/when it's a comfortable temperature for the mice / it's very difficult to heat a well-ventilated cage so it won't be suitable for other times of year/when it's colder *[1 mark]*.

It's a good idea to make sure you've understood how every point from the market research affects the design brief. Then you can make suitable changes to the design brief based on all of the market research rather than just one point. For example, you may be tempted to change the brief to a cage that is only designed for indoor use. However, only 18% of owners would keep their mice indoors all the time if they had a choice, so there is a market for a cage that can be used outside.

Section Eight

Pages 94-95 — Market Research

1 a) i) The group of people you want to sell a product to *[1 mark]*.
   ii) Any two from: e.g. by their gender / their job / their hobbies / the amount of money they earn *[2 marks]*.
  b) E.g. male professionals *[1 mark]* because it's a man's suit and is most likely to appeal to men who wear suits every day to work *[1 mark]*.

2 a) The product would need to be designed to hold at least 5 games *[1 mark]* and to hold the most common size of game (19 cm x 14 cm) *[1 mark]*.
  b) Closed question: e.g. how much money would you spend on a carry case for computer games?
   A: less than £5, B: £5-10, C: £10-15, D: more than £15
   [1 mark]
   Open question: e.g. how do you transport your computer games at the moment? *[1 mark]*
  c) E.g. 100% = 360° so 1% = 360 ÷ 100 = 3.6°
   so angle of sector (less than once) = 3.6 × 32 = 115.2°
   (or 115° to the nearest degree).
   OR angle of sector (once) = 3.6 × 36 = 129.6°
   (or 130° to the nearest degree).

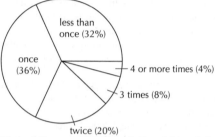

   [1 mark for correct angle calculated, 1 mark for accurately completed pie chart]
   You only need to calculate the angle of one of the two sectors — once you've plotted one, the other is the sector that's left over. You could use this leftover sector to check your answer though — just calculate the angle it should be and check this matches what you've got on your chart.
  d) i) E.g. interviews give you the chance to ask follow-up questions which questionnaires don't / to get more detailed information than questionnaires *[1 mark]*.
   ii) E.g. they allow the interview to be analysed at a later date / the interviewer doesn't need to take notes, which can stop the flow of conversation *[1 mark]*.
   iii) E.g. to generate a guided discussion, where members can freely give their opinions to questions that have been prepared in advance *[1 mark]*.

Pages 96-97 — Product Analysis

Warm-up
True, False, True
1 a) Product 1: e.g. it is made from a good thermal insulator/plastic, so won't get very hot/is safe to use / product 1 has no scale to read the water level *[1 mark]*.
   Product 2: e.g. the base is made from metal, so it may get hot easily/present a risk of burning the user / product 2 has a scale that allows the customer to see how much water is inside easily *[1 mark]*.
  b) Product 1: e.g. it is light-coloured and should fit in well with most other kitchen equipment / has a very chunky-looking handle which isn't attractive / has a boring design *[1 mark]*.
   Product 2: e.g. it has a modern/sleek appearance / is attractive because you can see the water boiling *[1 mark]*.
  c) Product 1: e.g. it has a chunky handle that might not be suitable for small hands to grip around / the handle doesn't leave much of a gap for large hands to fit into *[1 mark]*.
   Product 2: e.g. it has a handle design that is suitable for a wide range of hand sizes, as it is only joined to the rest of the kettle at the top *[1 mark]*.
2 a) E.g. the coat has a water-resistant finish, which makes it suitable for wet weather *[1 mark]*. However, it isn't padded so it might not be warm enough for winter *[1 mark]*.

  b) E.g. the coat is made out of nylon/the buttons are made out of plastic, which is cheap to buy *[1 mark]*. However, the metal brooch will increase the cost of the coat *[1 mark]*.
  c) E.g. nylon/plastic is made from fossil fuels, which are finite resources/will eventually run out, so it isn't a sustainable material *[1 mark]*. However, the plastic buttons have been recycled, which makes it more environmentally friendly *[1 mark]*.
  d) E.g. bad/unsafe working conditions *[1 mark]* / paying workers unfairly *[1 mark]*.

Page 98 — Design Strategies

Warm-up
Systems approach — A design strategy that involves breaking down the design process into a number of different stages, and doing each one in turn.
User-centred design — A design strategy in which the wants and needs of the user are prioritised throughout the design process.
Design fixation — A situation where the designer gets stuck on a particular idea when designing a product.
1 Any two from: e.g. clients *[1 mark]* — this allows feedback to be gathered on whether the design/model/prototype fits with what the clients had in mind, so improvements can be made that suit the clients' wants/needs *[1 mark]*. / Users/target market *[1 mark]* — this allows feedback to be gathered on what potential users like/dislike about the design, so improvements can be made to make the product more appealing to them *[1 mark]*. / Experts/industry professionals *[1 mark]* — this allows the designer to benefit from their experience in the industry / allows the designer to get technical feedback about the design *[1 mark]*.
2 How to grade your answer:
   [No marks] There is no relevant information.
   [1 mark] There is a brief description of the process, but key stages are left out and the answer contains a number of errors. AND/OR there is a diagram but it lacks detail and clarity.
   [2 marks] There is a description of the process, but some points are missing or there are some errors. AND/OR there is a diagram with some annotations, but it lacks detail or contains errors.
   [3 marks] There is a detailed description of the process, with most stages in the correct order but the description may contain small errors or lack some clarity. AND/OR there is an annotated diagram, which is mainly correct but some points are missing.
   [4 marks] There is a clear, accurate and detailed description of the process, including the key stages in the correct order. AND/OR there is an accurate and appropriately annotated diagram clearly showing the process.
   Here are some points your answer may include:
   Develop a design brief and specification.
   Sketch and model design ideas.
   Make a prototype.
   Hold a focus group for the prototype to be tested by the target market / test the prototype yourself.
   Evaluate the design / identify any problems based on testing/feedback.
   Improve the design to fix any problems.
   Make another prototype.
   Continue making new and improved prototypes by repeating the same method until all the problems have been identified and fixed.
   (Relevant, labelled sketches with annotations showing these points should also be credited.)

Pages 99-100 — Exploring and Developing a Design Idea

1 a) Any two from: e.g. to try out different materials in a design / to try out different joining techniques / to try out designs that reduce the number of parts/make construction easier *[2 marks]*.
  b) E.g. jelutong/balsa *[1 mark]*, because it's cheap / easy to work / quick to produce a model *[1 mark]*.
  c) e.g. a breadboard *[1 mark]*
2 a) The toile could be put on a mannequin/tried on by the client *[1 mark]* to work out the proportions and fit of the dress *[1 mark]*.

Section Eight

b) i) E.g. cheap *[1 mark]* — so the design can be experimented with/ improved without costing too much/without wasting the real fabric *[1 mark]*. / Lightly coloured *[1 mark]* — so changes can be marked up onto it *[1 mark]*.

ii) e.g. calico/unbleached cotton *[1 mark]*

3 a) the design specification *[1 mark]*

b) E.g. test that the carton holds 200 ml of milk / test that the foil cover is easy enough to break with a straw / test that the straw fits through the hole / test that the carton doesn't leak *[1 mark]*.

c) E.g. the star shape is complex and may be difficult to manufacture/assemble *[1 mark]*. The carton could be made in a simpler shape, such as a rectangular box, to reduce manufacturing costs *[1 mark]*.

d) making a prototype *[1 mark]*

Pages 101-102 — Drawing Techniques

1 a) They are used to show 3D pictures of objects at 30° *[1 mark]*.

b) E.g.

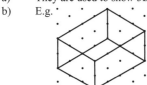

Correct shape *[1 mark]*
Correct dimensions *[1 mark]*

2 a) E.g. a flowchart that separates a system into input, process and output boxes *[1 mark]*.

b) E.g. schematic diagrams clearly show the layout of a system *[1 mark]* whereas system diagrams are used to outline the basic design/concept of the system *[1 mark]*.

c) e.g. a circuit diagram / a diagram in a repair manual *[1 mark]*

d) E.g. because they are designed to be easy to read *[1 mark]* and simple to draw *[1 mark]*.

3 a) It shows what something actually looks like in 3D — smaller in the distance, larger close up *[1 mark]*.

b) E.g.

Original shape drawn using one-point perspective *[1 mark]*.
Accurate drawing with neat lines *[1 mark]*.

c) E.g.

Original shape drawn using two-point perspective *[1 mark]*.
Correctly positioned above the horizon *[1 mark]*.
Accurate drawing with neat lines *[1 mark]*.

Pages 103-104 — More on Drawing Techniques

1 a) Name: exploded diagram *[1 mark]*
Explanation: because it shows how the parts of a product fit together *[1 mark]*.

b) E.g.

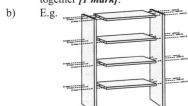

Accurate reproduction of the bookcase exploded *[1 mark]*.
Each part of the bookcase is in line with the part it's attached to *[1 mark]*.
Dotted lines show where parts explode from *[1 mark]*.

2 a) Width of the table = 1.25 m = 125 cm *[1 mark]*
Scale of the drawing = 25 : 125 = 1 : 5 *[1 mark]*

The measurements need to be in the same units (e.g. cm) before you write them as a ratio. 25 : 125 is simplified by dividing both sides by 25.

b) 18 × 5 = 90 cm *[1 mark]*

The 1 : 5 ratio can be read as "scale drawing size : real object size", so the height of the table is 5 times larger than its height in the scale drawing.

3 a) i) plan view *[1 mark]*
ii) end view *[1 mark]*

b) E.g.

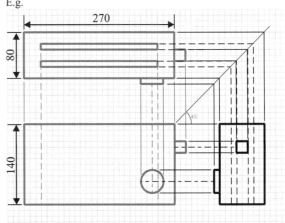

End view is drawn correctly *[1 mark]*.
Hidden details are drawn correctly *[1 mark]*.
Dimensions are labelled correctly *[1 mark]*.

Pages 105-106 — Manufacturing Specification

1 a) E.g.

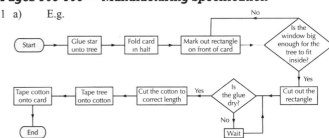

All processes given with a rectangular box drawn around each one *[1 mark]*.
Processes are listed in a practical order *[1 mark]*.
A suitable quality control check in a diamond-shaped box with 'yes' and 'no' arrows coming out of it is included *[1 mark]*.

b) Any two from: e.g. how much of each material will be needed / precise dimensions of the window / the tolerances of the window dimensions / any finishing details / costings *[2 marks]*.

2 a) Any two from: e.g. the type of fabric to be used / the precise amount of fabric needed / the fabric colour / any fabric finish needed *[2 marks]*.

b) Any two from: e.g. clear construction details / the equipment needed / the precise dimensions of each part / tolerances of each part / quality control instructions / a breakdown of all the costs *[2 marks]*.

3 a) Gantt chart *[1 mark]*

b) i) 10 minutes *[1 mark]*

The row of the chart that involves painting the box has two shaded squares. Each square is worth 5 minutes, so it should take 10 minutes to complete.

ii) 80 minutes *[1 mark]*

c) E.g. paint the lid before painting the box, to allow the labels to be applied while the box is drying *[1 mark]*.

To make the manufacturing process quicker, the order in which the tasks are completed needs to change so that there is more overlap between tasks.

Pages 107-108 — Developing Prototypes

Warm-up
False, True, False

1 Any three from: e.g. to check the manufacturing specification for the tent is correct / to help calculate the manufacturing costs / to test that the tent meets the design specification / to get feedback from other people/the client/potential customers/experts in the industry *[3 marks]*.

2 The label does show the name of the product *[1 mark]* but not what it smells of *[1 mark]*. It has an old-fashioned rather than

Answers

futuristic/scientific appearance *[1 mark]*. It doesn't include an image of glossy hair *[1 mark]*.

3 a) It must appeal to children — e.g. the black colour probably won't appeal to children *[1 mark]*.
It must be highly visible for road safety purposes — e.g. the coat is dark so isn't easy to see *[1 mark]*.

b) E.g. make the coat a brighter colour/more than one colour so that it would be more appealing to children *[1 mark]*.
E.g. make the coat from a material that is highly visible colour instead of black / add reflective stripes to the coat *[1 mark]*.

c) E.g. a new prototype could be made with the suggested improvements *[1 mark]*. This new prototype could then be tested/evaluated *[1 mark]*.

d) When the prototype is as perfect as it can be *[1 mark]*.

Pages 109-110 — Using Materials Efficiently

Warm-up
Odd-leg caliper — Marks a line parallel to an edge.
Try square — Helps to accurately mark out right angles.
Scriber — Used like a pencil to scratch a mark into metal and plastic.
Tailor's chalk — Used to transfer markings onto a fabric that you can remove later.
Templates — Drawn around to mark out the same shape.

1 a) nesting / lay planning *[1 mark]*
b) E.g. to save money *[1 mark]* and to reduce harm to the environment *[1 mark]*.
c) Because the shapes will fit together without any gaps or overlapping pieces *[1 mark]*, meaning less of each sheet of material will be thrown away *[1 mark]*.
d) E.g.

Hexagons should be drawn with no gaps. At least one hexagon should be completely surrounded by other hexagons *[1 mark]*.

One of the hexagons needs to be drawn completely surrounded by other hexagons to show that it tessellates on all sides of the shape.

2 E.g. marking out helps to make sure products are cut accurately and within the required tolerance *[1 mark]*.
This reduces waste as incorrectly sized products would have to be thrown away *[1 mark]*.

3 Total volume of material = $5 \times 5 \times 240 = 6000$ cm^3 *[1 mark]*
So material wasted = $6000 - 5775 = 225$ cm^3 *[1 mark]*

4 a)

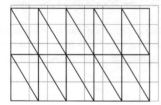

[1 mark]

b) Area = $\frac{1}{2} \times 15 \times 24 = 180$ cm^2 *[1 mark]*
Area of a triangle = ½ × width × height.

c) Area of sheet = $80 \times 50 = 4000$ cm^2 *[1 mark]*
Area of 20 triangles = $180 \times 20 = 3600$ cm^2 *[1 mark]*
So material wasted = $4000 - 3600 = 400$ cm^2 *[1 mark]*

Page 111 — Working Safely

1 Any two from: e.g. he should wear chainmail gloves / wear ear protection / remove his watch / secure the wood he is cutting with a clamp / use a dust extractor / wear a dust mask / wear eye protection *[2 marks]*.

2 a) i) e.g. a thimble *[1 mark]*
ii) e.g. ear protection *[1 mark]*
iii) e.g. dust mask / goggles *[1 mark]*
b) e.g. make sure there is adequate ventilation *[1 mark]*
c) Any two from: e.g. make sure sleeves are rolled back / make sure ties are tucked in/taken off / make sure apron strings are tucked in / make sure necklaces/watches/rings are taken off / make

sure long hair is tied back / never leave a machine unattended when on / never use a machine unless you've been taught how to / know how to switch a machine off in an emergency / don't change parts on a machine until it's isolated from the mains / secure work safely / use guards on machines that have them / use a dust extractor if the process produces dust *[2 marks]*.

3 Hazard: e.g. working with hot materials *[1 mark]*
Precaution: e.g. wear protective gloves / an apron / a tinted face shield *[1 mark]*.

Section Nine — Mixed Questions

Pages 112-124 — Mixed Questions

1 B *[1 mark]*
2 D *[1 mark]*
3 B *[1 mark]*
4 C *[1 mark]*
5 A *[1 mark]*
6 Process:
Plastic packaging tray — e.g. vacuum forming
Cotton fabric — e.g. plain weaving
Cogs in watch mechanism — e.g. laser cutting
Printed wallpaper — e.g. flexography *[1 mark]*
How to grade your answer:
[No marks] There is no relevant information.
[1 mark] There is a brief description of the process, but key stages are left out and the answer contains a number of errors. AND/OR there is a diagram but it lacks detail and clarity.
[2 marks] There is a description of the process, but some points are missing or there are some errors. AND/OR there is a diagram with some annotations, but it lacks detail or contains errors.
[3 marks] There is a detailed description of the process, with most stages in the correct order but the description may contain small errors or lack some clarity. AND/OR there is an annotated diagram, which is mainly correct but some points are missing.
[4 marks] There is a clear, accurate and detailed description of the process, including the key stages in the correct order. AND/OR there is an accurate and appropriately annotated diagram clearly showing the process.
Here are some points your answer may include:
Plastic packaging:
A mould of the tray is put onto a vacuum bed.
A film/sheet of thermoforming plastic is clamped above the vacuum bed.
The plastic sheet/film is heated until it goes soft.
The vacuum bed is lifted close to the heated plastic.
Air is sucked out from under the plastic, creating a vacuum and forcing the plastic onto the mould of the tray.
The moulded plastic is cooled and the vacuum bed lowered.
The cold plastic is rigid so holds the shape of the tray.
Cotton fabric:
A loom is used to weave cotton yarns into a fabric.
Cotton fabrics are woven by interlacing a weft yarn and a warp yarn.
The weft travels from right to left and the warp yarn travels up and down the weave.
The yarns are interlaced by passing the weft yarn over and under alternate warp yarns to create a plain weave.
Looms can be operated by hand or computer-controlled.
Cogs in watch mechanism:
The cog is designed on a computer using computer-aided design (CAD) software.
The correct feed rate values and power settings are programmed into the laser cutter.
The type and thickness of the material being used determine the feed rate and power settings needed.
A laser beam cuts through the material to accurately cut out the exact shape of a cog.
The laser is guided using computer numeric control (CNC) — it follows the coordinates set out in the design.

Printed wallpaper:
The printing plate is made from flexible rubber/plastic.
The striped pattern sticks out a bit from the plate.
Paint is applied to the raised areas of the printing plate.
The printing plate is rolled over the wallpaper to transfer the striped pattern to the paper.
(Relevant, labelled sketches with annotations showing these points should also be credited.)

7   B *[1 mark]*

8   A *[1 mark]*

9   A book cover:
Finish/treatment: e.g. embossing *[1 mark]*
Description: e.g. a shaped die is pushed into the back of the material to leave a slightly raised impression on its surface *[1 mark]*.
Reason for choice: e.g. it's often used to draw attention to a particular bit of a product, e.g. the title of a book *[1 mark]*.
A garden shed:
Finish/treatment: e.g. tanalising *[1 mark]*
Description: e.g. timber is placed in a tank which is flooded with preservative and then pressurised to force the preservative deep into the wood *[1 mark]*.
Reason for choice: e.g. the treatment helps to prevent insect attacks and the decay of the wood, meaning it will last longer *[1 mark]*.
The metal handle of a tool:
Finish/treatment: e.g. dip coating *[1 mark]*
Description: e.g. a metal is heated evenly in an oven before being plunged into fluidised powder. It is then returned to the oven, which causes the thin layer of plastic to fuse to the surface of the handle *[1 mark]*.
Reason for choice: e.g. it offers a soft, smooth finish for tool handles *[1 mark]*.
A 2000 metre roll of plain cotton:
Finish/treatment: e.g. industrial flat-bed screen printing *[1 mark]*
Description: e.g. fabric passes under screens, each filled with a different colour of dye, on a conveyor belt and the colours are applied one after the other *[1 mark]*.
Reason for choice: e.g. this method allows very long lengths of fabric to be printed on quickly *[1 mark]*.
A printed circuit board (PCB) in an air conditioning unit located outdoors:
Finish/treatment: e.g. PCB lacquering *[1 mark]*
Description: e.g. PCB lacquer is a thin polymer film that is sprayed or painted on to a PCB, or is applied by dipping the whole board into it *[1 mark]*.
Reason for choice: e.g. the lacquer provides a protective barrier against moisture, chemicals, large temperature changes and dust, which might be encountered by the PCB as it is situated outdoors *[1 mark]*.

10 a)   E.g.

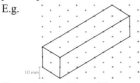

Correct shape *[1 mark]*
Correct dimensions *[1 mark]*

b) i)   81.5 mm *[1 mark]*
ii)   The width of the box is too small *[1 mark]*, as it needs to be between 18.5 mm and 21.5 mm / has a tolerance of 20 ± 1.5 mm *[1 mark]*.
iii)   The mark shows that the printing plates are not aligned correctly *[1 mark]* as the mark is not a single, clear image *[1 mark]*.

c) i)   a template *[1 mark]*
ii)   Area of sheet = 594 × 841 = 499 554 mm² *[1 mark]*
Area of 25 nets = 19 200 × 25 = 480 000 mm² *[1 mark]*
So material wasted = 499 554 − 480 000 = 19 554 mm² *[1 mark]*

d) i)   Height of the box = 1.5 m = 150 cm *[1 mark]*
Scale of the drawing = 15 : 150 = 1 : 10 *[1 mark]*
The 15 : 150 ratio is simplified by dividing both sides of the ratio by 15.

ii)   390 ÷ 10 = 39 cm *[1 mark]*
Award a mark if the correct calculation was done using an incorrect answer given in part i).

11 a)   E.g. upholstered bed frames are more popular than metal or wood frames / metal bed frames are more popular than wood frames / wood frames are the least popular of the options available *[1 mark]*.

b)   Q2: e.g. the bed should be designed to have some storage built in *[1 mark]*.
Q3: e.g. the bed should be designed to be a double bed *[1 mark]*.

c)   Total number of people who expect to spend £150 or less on a bed = 41 + 152 + 113 = 306
(306 ÷ 360) × 100 = 85% *[1 mark]*

d)   E.g.

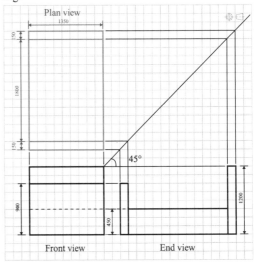

End view is drawn correctly *[1 mark]*.
Front view is correctly drawn *[1 mark]*.
Hidden detail is drawn correctly *[1 mark]*.
900 mm dimension is drawn and labelled correctly *[1 mark]*.
450 mm dimension is drawn and labelled correctly *[1 mark]*.
1200 mm dimension is drawn and labelled correctly *[1 mark]*.
A third angle orthographic projection is a scale drawing, so you'll need to draw the other two views with the scale that is used for the plan view. From the plan view you know that 1 grid square represents 150 mm, so you can use this to draw the other views to scale — e.g. 900 mm is 900 ÷ 50 = 6 squares.

e)   e.g. height of target market *[1 mark]*

f)   Any two from: e.g. materials can be bought in bulk / the initial cost of equipment is spread over a large number of products / workers on lower wages can be used as they don't need to be highly skilled / automated processes/robots can replace human workers on an assembly line, so less wages need to be paid / automation can increase speed of production / automation reduces human error, which can be costly *[2 marks]*.

12 a)   compression *[1 mark]*

b)   E.g. HDPE/plastic is made from crude oil, which is a non-renewable resource, whereas wood is a renewable resource. / HDPE/plastics are generally not biodegradable, whereas wood is *[2 marks]*.

c)   Any two from: e.g. the blocks should be brightly coloured *[1 mark]* so that they appeal to young children *[1 mark]*. / The blocks must be durable *[1 mark]* so that they last for a long time *[1 mark]*. / The blocks must be weatherproof *[1 mark]* so they don't become damaged by being outdoors *[1 mark]*. / The blocks shouldn't have sharp edges *[1 mark]* so they are safe for young children to use *[1 mark]*.
There are loads of different things that you could write to answer this question — just make sure that you can back up each of your suggested design criteria with a good reason.

d) i)   A full-size, fully-functioning product or system *[1 mark]* made to test the product/system and its production methods *[1 mark]*.
ii)   E.g. the dimensions of the blocks could be reduced *[1 mark]* to make them easier for children to hold/easier to store *[1 mark]*.

The set could include pieces of different shapes *[1 mark]* to allow more structures to be built/to make it more interesting *[1 mark]*.

   iii) E.g. experts in the industry *[1 mark]*

13   How to grade your answer:

[No marks] There is no relevant information.

[1 mark] There is a brief description of the work of one of the named designers. The answer may contain major errors and lack relevant detail.

[2 marks] There is a description of the work one of the named designers. Some key facts about the designer's work are covered but the answer lacks the detail needed to give a clear understanding. Some minor errors may be present.

[3 marks] There is a clear description of the work one of the named designers. The answer doesn't contain any errors and gives enough key facts to provide an accurate impression of the work of the designer's work.

For this question you <u>must</u> talk about the work of one of the designers listed in the question. There's a huge variety of things that you could say to answer this question, so we've just given advice on how marks would be awarded rather than any specific points to include.

14   <u>Standard component:</u>

Paper catalogue — e.g. comb binding

Wooden cupboard — e.g. butt hinge

Coat — e.g. zip

Bicycle — e.g. roller chain *[1 mark]*

How to grade your answer:

[No marks] There is no relevant information.

[1 mark] There is a brief description of how the named component is used, but some details are left out and the answer contains a number of errors. AND/OR there is a diagram but it lacks detail and clarity.

[2 marks] There is a detailed description of how the named component is used, but with some errors. AND/OR there is well-annotated diagram, but there are some errors.

[3 marks] There is a clear, accurate and detailed description of how the named component is used, including key details. AND/OR there is a clear, accurate and appropriately annotated diagram showing how the named component is used.

15 a)   E.g. a metal *[1 mark]* because metals are good conductors of electricity *[1 mark]*.

  b)   E.g. this is the part of the gloves that will be used to touch the screen *[1 mark]*.

  c) i) B = 40.00 ÷ 1000 = £0.04

C = 202.50 ÷ 2250 = £0.09 *[1 mark]*

    ii) E.g. length of thread needed for one pair of gloves in metres = 65 ÷ 100 = 0.65 m *[1 mark]*

Thread length needed to make 7000 pairs of gloves = 0.65 m × 7000 = 4550 m *[1 mark]*

Length of thread on a cone from supplier A is 1650 m, so the number of cones needed to give enough thread is 4550 ÷ 1650 = 2.76 which means that 3 cones are needed. Each cone costs £246.50, so the total cost of thread needed = 3 × £246.50 = £739.50 *[1 mark]*

Thread is only available in whole cones, so you'd need to buy 3 cones to have enough thread to make 7000 pairs of gloves.

    iii) E.g. when shipments of the thread are transported, fossil fuels are burnt *[1 mark]*, which releases greenhouse gases into the atmosphere *[1 mark]*. These greenhouse gases contribute to the carbon footprint of the gloves *[1 mark]*. Fewer shipments results in lower greenhouse gas emissions, therefore reducing the carbon footprint of the gloves *[1 mark]*.

  d) i) E.g. they will keep the users' hands warm in cold conditions *[1 mark]*.

    ii) Wool — sheep's fleece *[1 mark]*

Synthetic polyamide — crude oil *[1 mark]*

    iii) Any two from: e.g. drilling for crude oil can result in toxic chemicals being released into the atmosphere / can result in waste material/oil leaks, which pollute the surrounding habitats / may require land to be cleared to make room for the drill site, which can destroy habitats *[2 marks]*.

    iv) How to grade your answer:

[No marks] There is no relevant information.

[1 mark] There is a brief description of the process, but key stages are left out and the answer contains a number of errors. AND/OR there is a diagram but it lacks detail and clarity.

[2 marks] There is a description of the process, but some points are missing or there are some errors. AND/OR there is a diagram with some annotations, but it lacks detail or contains errors.

[3 marks] There is a detailed description of the process, with most stages in the correct order but the description may contain small errors or lack some clarity. AND/OR there is an annotated diagram, which is mainly correct but some points are missing.

[4 marks] There is a clear, accurate and detailed description of the process, including the key stages in the correct order. AND/OR there is an accurate and appropriately annotated diagram clearly showing the process.

Here are some points your answer may include:

<u>Sheep's fleece:</u>

The sheep is sheared to gather the wool.

The best wool comes from the sheep's shoulders and sides.

The wool is cleaned and scoured (washed with harsh chemicals) which removes grease and dried sweat.

The fibres are then combed using wire rollers (carding).

The fibres are then spun into yarn.

<u>Crude oil:</u>

Crude oil is fractionally distilled.

Certain chemicals are joined together to make polymers (polyamide).

The polymer is then melted and forced through tiny holes to form long filaments.

The filaments are left to cool, before being spun into yarn.

(Relevant, labelled sketches with annotations showing these points should also be credited.)

  e) i) The 50th percentile *[1 mark]*.

    ii) Any two from: e.g. hand width / finger length / thumb length / hand thickness *[2 marks]*

16 a)   E.g. the lamp has a traditional/antique appearance. / The lamp is decorative. / The lamp uses a design inspired by nature *[1 mark]*.

  b) i) one-off production *[1 mark]*

    ii) E.g. recycling generally uses less energy than obtaining new materials, so recycled glass has a lower carbon footprint than new glass *[1 mark]*. Using recycled glass may also avoid some glass going to waste and polluting the environment by taking up space in landfill *[1 mark]*.

    iii) alloy *[1 mark]*

TAQA41   £2.00
(Retail Price)

www.cgpbooks.co.uk